# the
# art of
# change

## a guided journal

# the
# art of
# change

*a guided journal*

## 8 Weeks to Making a Meaningful Shift in Your Life

## NANCY LEVIN

**HAY HOUSE, INC.**
Carlsbad, California • New York City
London • Sydney • New Delhi

**Published in the United States by:** Hay House, Inc.: www.hayhouse.com®
**Published in Australia by:** Hay House Australia Pty. Ltd.: www.hayhouse.com.au
**Published in the United Kingdom by:** Hay House UK, Ltd.: www.hayhouse.co.uk
**Published in India by:** Hay House Publishers India: www.hayhouse.co.in

*Cover design:* Karla Baker
*Interior design:* Julie Davison

**Cataloging-in-Publication Data is on file at the Library of Congress**

Tradepaper ISBN: 978-1-4019-6916-5

10  9  8  7  6  5  4  3  2  1
1st edition, September 2022

Printed and bound in Great Britain by
TJ Books Limited, Padstow, Cornwall.

# phases
## of the
# journey

# Start Here

## Dear Brave Explorer,

I'm so glad you're joining me here! *The Art of Change: A Guided Journal—8 Weeks to Making a Meaningful Shift* is for truth seekers and curious souls who are ready to make a shift in a short period of time— and to become skilled practitioners in the art of change. This guided journal will show you that making change is, indeed, an art—and it's nowhere near as hard as most of us might believe.

As the founder of Levin Life Coach Academy, I've been over-joyed to guide hundreds of aspiring and existing coaches—and thou-sands of clients—through a multifaceted journey that supports their evolution and enhances their personal and professional life. To that end, I've developed a number of tools, prompts, and proven processes that can help people change their lives and align with the most fulfill-ing, exciting, and authentic vision they hold for themselves.

Needless to say, I am a huge believer in the power of coaching. A number of studies have revealed that coaching is an effective way to facilitate the attainment of our goals and create a greater sense of purpose and meaning. It offers people a framework for commitment, accountability, support, and receptivity to powerful insights. I'm not exaggerating when I say that I've seen lives permanently transformed through coaching—including my own.

While having a coach who's there to witness your struggles and triumphs, and to help guide life-changing realizations, can be a rich and meaningful part of the process, I decided to create this guided journal because I want to offer you the next best thing: a space for self-inquiry, discovery, and reflection that will empower you to bring about the changes you want. First and foremost, the change I'm talking about begins with the way you see yourself and what you're capable of.

Just like any committed coach, I'll be with you every step of the way, guiding you in the direction of your reinvention: a return to the essence of who you are instead of endless versions of who you think you need to be. By dissolving the obstacles in your way, you can tap into your desire and discover the power available to you for creating lasting change. When it comes down to it, change begins with your commitment to your own evolution. It also requires that you honor the space between "no longer" and "not yet," even as you are in the space of "becoming." When you practice the *eight dimensions of reinvention,* which we'll explore together over the next eight weeks, you can embody the art of change by consciously curating what you want to bring into your life and what you want to release.

> **Reinvention: a return to the essence of who you are instead of endless versions of who you think you need to be.**

The teachings and exercises in *The Art of Change* will let you dip your toes into the ocean of change and dive in as deeply as you want to. You'll explore the eight dimensions of reinvention through bite-sized, actionable daily prompts designed to take you into the deepest archaeological dig possible: the one that leads to the heart of who you are.

Each week, we'll journey through one of the eight dimensions of reinvention:

- **Vision:** Your vision is the touchstone that determines the choices you make and the actions you take.

- **Calibration:** Having a powerful vision for change requires the ability to continuously assess your journey and course-correct when you need to.

- **Beliefs:** What ultimately holds you back is what you believe about yourself—which is why it's a good idea to dig deep and uncover any hidden beliefs.

- **Self-Worth:** If you believe you're not enough, you'll also believe there isn't enough or you'll never have enough. This gets shattered when you recognize that your worth is inherent.

- **Boundaries:** By firmly setting and holding your boundaries, you'll move out of blame and victimhood, and into responsibility and empowerment, as you build a stronger relationship with yourself.

- **Choice:** Every choice you make either serves or sabotages you. Your present-moment choices predict your future—so if you don't make conscious choices to support your vision, your future will end up looking a lot like your past or present.

- **Self-Confidence:** When you shift from the need for external validation and approval, you discover a limitless source of self-confidence. And when you chip away at the personas and roles you've been taught to take on, you reclaim the extraordinary person who's buried beneath.

- **Visibility:** Visibility is all about allowing yourself to be seen in the truth of who you are. Once you own and honor visibility, you claim the courage to make the changes that will lead toward greater happiness, fulfillment, and purpose—and change becomes a natural part of your journey.

Because this journal is rooted in my work as a coach, I want to note that coaching is ultimately about moving from where you are now to where you want to be. As I mentioned above, change begins with your commitment to your own evolution. And with this journal, I'm committed to holding you accountable to the commitment you've made to yourself.

I suggest keeping a regular schedule with this journal: For example, you can read a new chapter on Sunday, and then take that week through Saturday to respond to the daily journal prompts. You can spend as much time as you'd like responding to each prompt (I recommend no less than 10 minutes, as this process is certain to unearth big realizations). The final prompt for the week will always be self-reflection on your overall experiences and observations with respect to the topic at hand.

Each week, you'll also identify actions you're committed to taking. You'll want to be sure that the actions you choose are realistic, manageable, and achievable. When we focus on a specific action, I want you to think in terms of *micro-action*. The bigger the action, the easier it is to self-sabotage by falling off track and throwing in the towel. The smaller micro-actions you create for yourself will support you in staying in alignment with your vision. This is not about running the whole marathon all at once. It's just about the next step. It's not even about the *right* step. It's not about right or wrong because we can always take an action in a direction and then course-correct. It's about movement, which mobilizes possibility.

In the first week, in addition to uncovering your vision, you'll also begin to orient toward centering your attention around yourself with rituals, routines, non-negotiables, and self-honoring practices. Perhaps you want to give up binge eating, rescuing others, or procrastinating on an important project by watching too much Netflix. Or maybe you have the desire to schedule a minimum of an hour a day just for you, or you want to go to sleep and wake up on a particular schedule. Think of what you need, the change you want to make, that will enable you to know you are worthy of love and care. Every week, after you've completed the daily journal prompts, you'll be exploring

> **It's just about the next step. It's not even about the *right* step. It's not about right or wrong because we can always take an action in a direction and then course-correct. It's about movement, which mobilizes possibility.**

and reflecting on these actions you've committed to, so you get in the habit of tracking yourself. Knowing that change requires you to pay attention to and honor yourself, let yourself select rituals and routines that will enable you to reconnect to *you*.

The reason you picked up this journal is that you want to experience positive change in your life. You want to step into a life that brings you a sense of deep joy and meaning, one in which you are accessing your full potential and expanding your capacity to recognize and live out your greatness! Think of this journal as being akin to a personal laboratory for your genius—a place where you can cultivate the skills and behaviors you need in order to get to where you want to go, as you chart and assess your progress along the way. Throughout it all, I'll be here to remind you to stay curious and cheer you on as you engage in this process of inquiry to return you to your essence.

Whether you're determined to shift a small habit or move massive mountains, *The Art of Change* will meet you where you are and take you where you want to go.

xo

# Vision

The central aspect of the art of change is the process of reinvention. Remember, reinvention isn't about scrubbing your life clean of any signs that you've lived it. It's about returning to the essence of who you actually are—the *you* that, quite possibly, has been hanging out beneath a mountain of habits, obligations, and inherited beliefs, gesturing wildly to get your attention: "Heyyyy, remember me?"

This is the *true you*—the inner spark that you sense when you're most at home in your body and your mind. It's the brightness that radiates out from you and touches everything you encounter; it makes colors more vivid and food tastier. It's the sense of passion and purpose you were born with, which gives life texture and meaning. In short, it's the essential part of you that makes life worth living.

Now, you might be thinking, *Well, that sounds nice, but it's definitely not my experience—at least not most of the time. So how can it possibly be the "true me"?*

I'm here to say that it is—even during the times you've lost direction, which is super easy to do if you're pinned beneath that gigantic mountain of patterns and behaviors you've come to identify as "me." In truth, who you are is infinite, which means it's not limited or defined by your life circumstances. In fact, the true self—which is calm, confident, and empowered—tends to become even more resilient when we are connected to it, because it isn't deterred by so-called obstacles or the litany of reasons to bury our heads in the sand and give up. In fact, when we live from the true self, we are inspired to discover creative solutions in the midst of pretty dismal situations. To use a cliché, we are inspired to turn lemons into lemonade because that's just part of our nature as human beings.

Unfortunately, we aren't often taught or encouraged by our society to dig deep and use this part of who we are as a vital resource to move us forward. We don't even know it's there half the time, much less that the true self is our superpower! This is why we have to be curious and courageous (and if you're here, reading this, I already know you are!). We must have the courage to embark on a journey of self-discovery that allows us to deeply explore our dreams, passions, and values; challenge limiting beliefs and ineffective habits that we've mistakenly taken at face value as "the way things are"; celebrate our true self as a magnificent being who is not fixed in space and time but is constantly evolving toward greater joy and contribution; and embrace our potential and purpose with enthusiasm and the willingness to learn and grow.

It's your birthright to live as your true self, but it takes practice to do so. At the foundation of this coaching journal, this practice will come by embracing my Transformation Equation:

# Change = Vision + Choice + Action

So, my fellow intrepid explorer, are you ready?

# Your Vision: Your True North

This week focuses on the first dimension of reinvention: vision. There's a reason that vision comes first in the Transformation Equation. Vision is the secret to creating real and lasting change. If you want change to occur, first you need to have a clear vision of where you want to go. Then you need to be willing to make different choices and take different actions.

When we set our course in alignment with our vision, it has the power to transform us. Vision becomes a gravitational force pulling us toward its fulfillment. Vision is essential to the journey. It becomes the map that guides our trajectory. Once we know where we're headed, we can make choices and take actions to support our vision. Every choice we make or action we take will either serve or sabotage our vision.

Here's what's so exciting about your vision: *It doesn't need to be created.* Just like your true self, your vision already exists within you. It is likely a bit dormant or dusty, or it has been neglected as other things got prioritized and pushed to the top of the to-do list—but your vision is still there! We're going to uncover it, unconceal it, and dust it off so it can actually get some fresh air and the light of our loving attention.

Why is knowing your vision so important? Well, because you simply cannot hope to become an effective practitioner of the art of change without identifying a fresh and clear vision that reflects your most authentic desires.

Many of us may feel disconnected from our vision because we have not plugged into our authentic desires. Even if we are not aware of it, we may be living someone else's version of what a "good," "normal," "stable," "successful" life looks like. A lot of times, a life that is bereft of a person's authentic desires may look like a life in which nothing ever feels good enough . . . or some vital but unidentifiable ingredient is missing, sapping our life of its spice and zest. If this is true for you, it's a sign you're disconnected from your own definitions of truth and success, or that you've taken on someone else's.

A powerful vision starts with powerful desires that actually move and excite you on a fundamental level. But if you've been disconnected from your desires for as long as you can remember, it's time to become present and still. It's time to give yourself the gift of your own undivided attention. So often, people are too busy being busy to check in with themselves, but this process requires your full permission to be here, now.

In fact, you may want to take a moment to slow down and put your hand over your heart as you simply feel into your body. Your body is the barometer of your truth. We tend to think we'll find answers in our head. We're so used to overriding our body and what we feel, but our feelings have a lot of important information for us when we stop to consider them. (If it isn't already obvious, you'll be invited to check in with your body and how you really feel throughout the course of this coaching journal. This means you are not to be perfunctory! No more telling yourself and others, "I'm fine," especially when that's probably not the case. I want you to take the time to be very specific about what's alive for you. Dig deep and be honest with yourself.)

The exercises in this section will give you permission to discover your desires and your vision, in all their glory. For now, I invite you to suspend needing to know *how* you're going to get from here to there—a preoccupation that can extinguish the fire of transformation before you've even begun the journey!

Right now, it's about opening up to *wanting* and *receiving*.

## Powered by Desire

One of the reasons we get so disconnected from our authentic desires (and thus, our authentic vision and authentic self) is that we're accustomed to tamping down our *wanting*. Often, we've already convinced ourselves we can't have what we want, or we put someone else's needs or desires ahead of our own. We're even taught that it's best to not have any *wants*—to be independent and self-sufficient, and to resist the need for help from the outside world. Also, we tend to get caught up in the fear that we can't have what we want, so why bother? We convince ourselves it would be too painful to want something we'll probably never end up getting. This is why, so often, when we do tap into a genuine desire, we dismiss it and give ourselves a long list of reasons why we aren't worthy of it or why other people deserve it more than we do. These are all tricks our mind plays to keep us from feeling the magnitude of our desires.

We also operate under the assumption that life is a zero-sum game: "If someone else has, I go without, or if I have, someone else goes without." We're trained to believe that desire is selfish—and that it's a bad or irresponsible thing! In truth, one of the greatest tools to support you on this journey is . . . selfishness. In fact, selfishness is the foundation for a great life. I'm talking about the kind of selfishness that fills your cup and allows you to ditch your people-pleasing ways, so you can get your own needs met. Until you know how to give yourself enough air, you'll always be gasping just to keep going. You might tend to fear being selfish to such a degree that you end up becoming selfless—which ultimately means that with each giving act, you vanish. You end up abandoning yourself and your own needs.

**Until you know how to give yourself enough air, you'll always be gasping just to keep going.**

Being selfish isn't about one-upping or exploiting others. It's about remembering the universe is an abundant place that's more than capable of giving all of us what we truly want and need. First, we have to become more comfortable with feeling and acknowledging desires—and recognizing that we are worthy of having them fulfilled. We have to fill our own pitcher before giving to anyone else, otherwise we're just giving from an ever-depleted vessel.

Sometimes, I have people come to me, exasperated, and say, "I've sat with this question of what I want for a really long time, and the answer is: I don't even know!" I would argue that every single person already innately knows what they desire, but as I've mentioned, they've repressed that knowing over time—to the extent that if you were to ask them about their favorite color, favorite food to eat, or their picture of a fulfilling life, they would draw a blank.

If you can relate, you're not alone! That was me for a long time too. But I want to emphasize that even if you draw a blank, it's okay! I'm not asking you to pull anything out of your imagination or fake it till you make it. Perhaps, like me, you're not necessarily much of a dreamer who spends your time creating vision boards and planning all the awesome things you're going to fill your life with. That's fine, because vision is actually less about dreaming and more about connecting to the passion you've been repressing and bringing it into your day-to-day.

This week, you're going to give yourself full permission to want. The daily prompts at the end of this section will enable you to go into specific areas of your life (which I chose because they're common themes that have arisen over and over among the thousands of people I've worked with), almost as if you are dividing your life into several slices of pie, so you can identify the vision that lives in that particular area. For the most thoroughness, be sure to spend at least 10 minutes on each daily prompt.

What you'll discover is that you're not being asked to come up with a blue-sky vision or a 10-year plan. When it comes to crafting a vision that moves us more decisively in the direction of what we want, it can be more manageable to do it step by step, inch by inch. By allowing your vision to be bite-sized, digestible, and manageable, you ensure that you don't overwhelm yourself. Taking incremental steps actually prepares you for the next step and sets you up to accomplish what you want. Procrastination is often the result of putting something off because it feels like it's "too big." In contrast, by getting connected to the very practical matter of what exactly needs to happen to move you closer to your desires, you end up building (and living!)

an integrated, holistic vision—which will be your map, as well as your compass, throughout the next eight weeks.

There is no right or wrong here. Your vision is 100 percent yours. It's your ideal set of circumstances that you have the power to activate when you take responsibility for what's in your control. As you go about discovering your vision, allow yourself to be in the presence of passion, desire, and dreaming, even if you have a knee-jerk aversion to wanting. Give yourself free rein. Remember, this process is just for you!

Of course, you may be aware of your inner critic judging you and offering a running commentary: *That's not very realistic now, is it? You don't have time to meditate every morning. You don't have money to hire that personal trainer. You're being selfish here.* It's helpful during this process to notice when that occurs, but not to let it deter you. I encourage you to allow this part of you to simply be a witness, a bystander to your process. Throughout the next few weeks, you'll begin neutralizing the witness so you can simply notice without putting the spin of good or bad, negative or positive, on what you observe. In this way, instead of spiraling into judgments, you can engage with your inner support system to stay in the witnessing energy with fascination and curiosity.

As you explore your vision this week, I invite you to stay in the "I." Remember, reinvention isn't about dusting off someone else's vision or modeling your vision on others'. It isn't about curating your world so that it looks like your favorite influencer's Instagram page. It's time to stop idealizing others and to begin inhabiting your own life on your own terms. Build a vision that allows you to step into the center stage of your own life!

# day 1: *health | physical, mental, emotional*

**In six months, my vision for my Health is:**

_____

_____

_____

_____

_____

_____

_____

_____

_____

_____

_____

In order for my vision
to be fulfilled, something
I can choose to integrate
into my life is:

In order for my vision
to be fulfilled, something
I can choose to eliminate
from my life is:

# day 2: *creativity*

## In six months, my vision for my Creativity is:

_____

_____

_____

_____

_____

_____

_____

_____

_____

_____

_____

_____

In order for my vision to be fulfilled, something I can choose to eliminate from my life is:

In order for my vision to be fulfilled, something I can choose to integrate into my life is:

# day 3:
relationships | intimate partnership, family, friends, business, other relationships

In six months, my vision for my Relationships is:

_____
_____
_____
_____
_____
_____
_____
_____
_____
_____
_____
_____

In order for my vision to be fulfilled, something I can choose to eliminate from my life is:

In order for my vision to be fulfilled, something I can choose to integrate into my life is:

# day 4: *career | mission | purpose | work in the world*

**In six months, my vision for my Career | Mission | Purpose | Work in the World is:**

_____

_____

_____

_____

_____

_____

_____

_____

_____

_____

In order for my vision
to be fulfilled, something
I can choose to integrate
into my life is:

In order for my vision
to be fulfilled, something
I can choose to eliminate
from my life is:

# day 5: *money*

In six months, my vision for my Money is:

_____
_____
_____
_____
_____
_____
_____
_____
_____
_____
_____

In order for my vision to be fulfilled, something I can choose to eliminate from my life is:

In order for my vision to be fulfilled, something I can choose to integrate into my life is:

# day 6: *adventure | pleasure | experience | fun*

**In six months, my vision for Adventure Pleasure | Experience | Fun is:**

_____

_____

_____

_____

_____

_____

_____

_____

_____

In order for my vision to be fulfilled, something I can choose to eliminate from my life is:

In order for my vision to be fulfilled, something I can choose to integrate into my life is:

# day 7: end-of-week reflections

## My Overall Vision

**This is what I experienced when uncovering my vision over the last week:**

_____

_____

_____

_____

_____

_____

_____

_____

_____

I was surprised by:

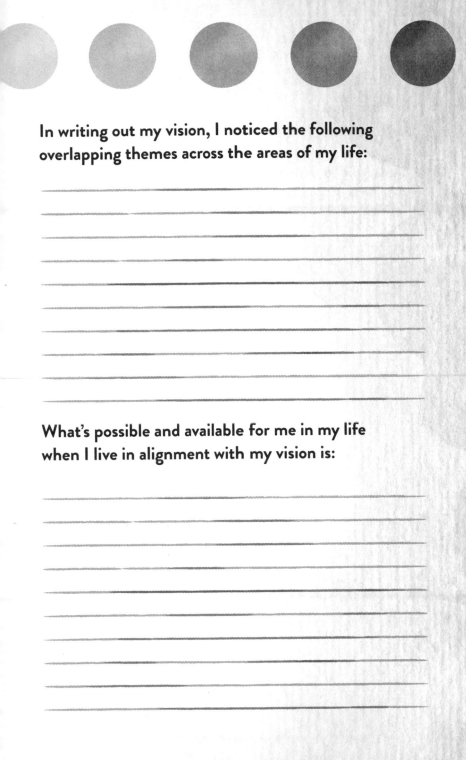

**In writing out my vision, I noticed the following overlapping themes across the areas of my life:**

_____

_____

_____

_____

_____

_____

_____

_____

_____

_____

**What's possible and available for me in my life when I live in alignment with my vision is:**

_____

_____

_____

_____

_____

_____

_____

_____

_____

_____

# self-honoring & non-negotiables

I will do this to connect with
myself in the morning:

I will do this to connect with
myself in the evening:

Now, identify one specific action you're willing to commit to this week. It might be something you are eliminating or adding to your life. It should be something specific you're committing to and willing to be held accountable for.

**One action I am choosing to take now to honor myself and reinvent my life is:**

**I acknowledge myself for:**

# Calibration

As we continue to delve into the Transformation Equation (Change = Vision + Choice + Action), we're going to explore the second dimension of reinvention: calibration. Becoming a skilled practitioner of the art of change isn't just about holding a vision and taking actions that move you closer toward that vision. It's about constantly noting any misalignments between your vision and your thoughts, words, behaviors, and actions.

What is calibration? It's the way we gauge, assess, and adjust as we move through the process of reinvention. It requires walking our selves through a practice of inquiry that allows us to get real with what is, and that lets us truly *presence* ourselves in our lives by taking stock of the good, the bad, the ugly, and everything in between. Calibration is an act of radical honesty that helps us course-correct when needed and to identify optimal pathways on the map of our vision.

Let's take a brief moment to calibrate, based on your experience of the last week. Take a few moments to attune to yourself. Imagine there is a meditation cushion inside your heart, waiting just for you. Take your seat and settle into your inner world. Now, let yourself look back at the past week and identify what served your reinvention. Did you take the action step you committed to? Did you propel yourself in the direction you want to go? What served your reinvention? Let yourself name it. Let yourself acknowledge it. Let yourself celebrate it. (Yes, celebration is part of calibration—notice how you only have to change two letters in each word to turn it into the other word?) With your next breath, notice what sabotaged your reinvention this past week. Perhaps it was the action you said you were going to take but didn't follow through with. Maybe it was negative self-talk, gossip, scrolling social media for longer than you would have liked, or something else. With your next breath, consider if you are honoring your commitment to yourself and your vision, along with your morning and evening routines of self-connection. Open your eyes and feel free to make some notes based on your observations.

_____

_____

_____

_____

_____

_____

_____

_____

_____

_____

All of the questions above are part of the process of calibration and moving into a state of inquiry that helps you to continually assess and reassess your vision, noting whether any part of how you're trying to fulfill that vision needs to be tweaked. Vision is your north star and your guidepost, and any choices or actions you take are meant to steer you closer to the life you know you want. You simply can't know if you're any closer to your goals if you don't assess and reassess your life to see if it's a testament to your vision. This is why it's necessary to continually calibrate the compass of your vision, which ensures that you're staying on course and maintaining your desired trajectory.

Often, it can be difficult to calibrate because we are not accurately assessing our lives as they are. We are out of alignment with what is, and we might be married to ideas about how we think our lives should be. Many of us are accustomed to thinking a certain way, or even *wanting* a certain way. This makes it likely that we're operating from an outdated version of ourselves we've outgrown or surpassed, but we haven't explicitly acknowledged the shift or replaced our old programming with new directives.

> **In many ways, self-sabotage is connected to the inability or unwillingness to calibrate and make small shifts when necessary.**

Calibration is very similar to a software update, or even a mental/emotional change of address. If you were indoctrinated with the idea that you need to be a doctor in order to be successful but eventually you realize you actually want to be a poet, you're not going to get very far until you update your operating system and align your choices and actions with the person you really are and desire to become more of.

In many ways, self-sabotage is connected to the inability or unwillingness to calibrate and make small shifts when necessary. We are conditioned to remain dogmatically attached to our vision, and if we "fail," we see this as a personal failure instead of considering that maybe we've placed too many obstacles in our own path and it's time to rethink our approach. It's time to calibrate.

# Moving Past Incompletions

Reinvention is a process of returning to your essence by constantly assessing and reassessing, calibrating and recalibrating. Now that you're learning to give yourself the gift of your own attention, you're going to be reading your life, your energy, and your desire in much the same way you would read a meter. And at any moment, you will hone your ability to be agile—to adjust, shift, and move in accordance with what is needed. You could define agility as the capacity to respond rapidly to change through adapting your own actions, habits, and behaviors. Think of how a martial artist quickly responds to an opponent's attack or counterattack: they aren't clinging to some plan for how their fighting "should" look; they're rolling with the punches and making their moves according to what's *actually* happening in the here and now.

Thing is, it's not possible to be agile, or to move forward in our lives, when we are weighed down by our past. So this week, we're going to calibrate by exploring what's holding us back. In the art of change, we call what's holding us back, weighing us down, and robbing us of our agility *incompletions*.

Incompletions are actions we didn't take in the past that create a barrier in the present, keeping us from the future we most desire. Incompletions are basically unfinished business: loose ends, neglected responsibilities, half-baked projects, and overlooked arrangements.

In the external world, incompletions can show up as broken agreements, clutter, lingering projects, old files, undone to-do lists, clothes that no longer fit, or anything lying around that we've literally and metaphorically outgrown—including jobs, relationships, and roles to which we've grown comfortably accustomed even though they may not fit the person we actually are.

We also have incompletions in our internal world. Incompletions can show up in our thoughts and emotions. They might manifest as grudges, resentments, strained relationships, beliefs and biases formed in the past, and old traumas.

In short, incompletions are the stuff we're still carrying with us that we have not put to rest. Some of these incompletions are things that we simply need to do in order to get closer to our vision; others are things we need to release because they're taking up too much mental and physical space, without actually serving us. A great way to locate incompletions is to pay attention to what you avoid, neglect, or procrastinate on.

Loyalty to our incompletions comes at the expense of our vision. Incompletions sap our energy and creativity, robbing us of focus and clarity and otherwise blocking us from creating the life we envision. We often allow our incompletions to drain us; we use them to beat ourselves up and dwell on our so-called failures; or we allow them to be yet another excuse to tamp down on our desire and convince ourselves that what we want is unattainable.

Our incompletions are at the root of our self-sabotage. They can hinder our ability to take action on things that need to be done. Many of us expend way too much energy hanging on to ideas, beliefs, roles, objects, and relationships that no longer serve us or fit the person we are, deep down. Often, we are living our lives with a surface-level connection to the truth, but we may be avoiding any kind of deeper, more soulful engagement with the truth, to the extent that we have grown used to lying to ourselves!

Unfortunately, we create chaos and unnecessary messes when we avoid the truth. When we align with what is true for us, we restore our energy from within and move toward nourishment. This is why it's so important that you fully inhabit your life and what is true for you, rather than continuing to be drained by outdated software—like your mother's dream that you would someday become a doctor.

As you can see, there's a big cost to incompletions—and that's why we want to clean them up this week!

In the next few days, you'll start looking at how incompletions show up in your life, externally and internally. You'll be able to see the cause and effect of how your external world is always a reflection of your internal world. The clutter that's happening externally is a direct reflection of the clutter that's happening internally.

Sometimes, we're aware of our incompletions. They are right in our faces or right in our awareness as we move through our days. And sometimes, our incompletions are a little hidden, murky, or covered up. Sometimes, we're not even aware of an incompletion until someone points it out to us, or it makes itself obvious and reveals just how much we need to change course.

We tend to avoid incompletions because they elicit feelings of guilt, shame, remorse, resentment, or blame. Here's the great news: Instead of running away from these uncomfortable emotions, we can see them as valuable information that's urging us to calibrate! These feelings can be an indication that something needs your attention; something needs to be addressed, completed, or released.

Even when an uncomfortable feeling arises, it's here as a guide. It serves as directional signage toward something you haven't been looking at, or that you've been avoiding or pushing away. Incompletions can be painful to face, especially since their associated emotions are not exactly pleasant—but we can reframe this perception so that we're encouraged to keep moving in the direction of our vision. When we start to see incompletions as nothing more than invitations to step into greater authenticity and freedom, it becomes easier to welcome them as opportunities for growth.

As you assess your incompletions, you'll also begin to connect and calibrate to choices and actions that are in alignment with your vision. That's because, when we address our incompletions by evaluating them, identifying our priorities, and cleaning up any old messes that unnecessarily consume our time and attention, this mobilizes movement and possibility. It frees us up for the future toward which we're attempting to move.

During the prompts for this week, it's likely that you'll be sorting through old stuff when addressing your incompletions. You might discover old projects or beliefs that it's time to close the loop on. It's also important to consider whether you're dragging an outdated incompletion around that you don't even want anymore. You might be so used to beating yourself up about something you haven't completed that you don't even realize it's no longer desired. So, as you uncover your incompletions, remember your vision: Is the incompletion still relevant to you? Is it still true for you? Is it necessary? Does it matter?

Is it still something you want or want to do? Don't worry too much about overthinking this process. Your vision is your north star, so it'll help you determine the obstacles that might be standing in your way. As long as you return to your vision to gauge where you are, the answers will reveal themselves.

As you go through this week's prompts, consider what you're willing to let go of now, and what no longer needs your attention even though at one time it may have felt really important. One of my poems includes the line, "A remembered truth is a dead thing." By this, I mean that even though that truth may have been something you held dearly in the past, it is no longer true and therefore no longer serves you. The process of calibrating and addressing your incompletions means you are giving yourself wholehearted permission to be with what's true *now* instead of hanging on to the past, or trying to make something that is no longer aligned with who you are fit into your life.

When we deal with our incompletions, we are essentially setting a boundary around what we are willing to live with and what we are not willing to live without. There are consequences to any boundary we set, which is why it can often be difficult to reach for the life we want if we're not ready to deal with the aftermath of setting our boundary!

Of course, this process is not about beating yourself up; it is about giving yourself permission to consciously choose to deal with an incompletion . . . or not. The key word is *conscious*. For example, if you don't feel ready or equipped to end a relationship that is not serving you, at the very least, you exercise awareness of this: "I'm staying put and I'm aware it's not in my best interest, but it's a choice I'm making right now." This is why calibration is so important—because it gives us the opportunity to come back to our incompletions, over and over again, and to make new choices based on where we are at the moment. However, an essential aspect of calibration is learning to forgive yourself if you realize you aren't ready to make certain changes.

The invocation of forgiveness might extend to other people in your life, as you consider incompletions in your relationships. Letting go of a grudge toward another person isn't about condoning their behavior or relieving them of responsibility. It's about giving yourself the gift of releasing the burden of resentment you've been carrying for so long, so you no longer continue to choose your own suffering. You can still make a choice around engaging with the other person, or not. But continuing to carry the resentment is a choice you make for *yourself*. Instead, consider choosing short-term discomfort over long-term resentment . . . especially when the person you often need to forgive most is yourself.

Before you get to this week's prompts, let's briefly explore any incompletions that may be bogging you down and compromising your agility. I invite you to take some slow, deep breaths. Let yourself digest everything you've been reading up until now. Allow yourself to connect with whatever feelings have come up so far.

With your next breath, bring into your awareness where in your life you feel most weighed down. It might be in relationships, career, money, or health; you can reflect on the categories and areas of your life we referenced to explore your vision. Identify the incompletions you have in these areas. Is there anything on this list of incompletions that no longer feels aligned with your vision?

> An essential aspect of calibration is learning to forgive yourself if you realize you aren't ready to make certain changes.

_____

_____

_____

Next, put your attention on any incompletions that *are* still aligned with your vision; what excuses do you use for why these things are not complete or why they're still festering in your internal world? What are you afraid will happen if you do them, clean them up, or let them go?

_____

_____

_____

Maybe you're afraid you'll have to really show up, or that you'll have to embrace success. Maybe cleaning up your incompletions means you won't get to play the victim anymore or carry around a sense of self-righteousness. Maybe you're afraid you'll have to rise into your purpose instead of remaining safe and small. What are you afraid will happen if you take responsibility here? Think of how much this costs you in terms of energy, self-esteem, happiness, health, peace of mind, and space.

You've clarified your vision, but the next steps of moving into choice and action won't be effective until you take time to calibrate and stay curious and open to what needs to change. Trust me when I say that most of us have many layers of incompletions. It's a lot easier to skim the surface and clean up what's easy and obvious, but it's harder to do the deeper dive and dig into the incompletions that bring up greater resistance. Don't beat yourself up over this—Rome wasn't built in a day. Think of it as an opportunity to keep calibrating, which will continue to give you chances to come back to those lingering incompletions!

Consider this a vital lesson in strength training; the more you clean up your incompletions, the more agile and adaptable you can be. The more agile and adaptable you are, the more present you become to what's true for you. The more present you are, the likelier it is that you'll set goals that actually resonate for you—so much so that you won't want to leave them incomplete!

# day 1

The places I feel weighed down in my life are:

_____

_____

_____

_____

_____

_____

_____

_____

_____

_____

_____

The incomplete or unfinished projects I have are:

_____

_____

_____

_____

_____

# day 2

The clutter and other things I am holding on to that
I no longer need, don't use, or that don't work are:

_____

_____

_____

_____

_____

_____

_____

The grudges, resentments, and broken agreements—
with myself or others—I am still feeling upset about are:

_____

_____

_____

_____

_____

_____

_____

# day 3

The excuses I use for why the things I wrote about in the last two days are not complete, not cleaned out, or still festering in my internal world are:

_____

_____

_____

_____

_____

_____

_____

The cost—in terms of energy, self-esteem, happiness, health, peace of mind, space, or in any other way—of having this unfinished business is:

_____

_____

_____

_____

_____

_____

_____

# day 4

If I take care of unfinished business, clean up
my incompletions, or let them go, I am afraid
this will happen:

_____
_____
_____
_____
_____
_____
_____
_____

The incompletion that is most sapping my energy
and creativity, robbing me of focus and clarity, or
otherwise blocking me from creating the life I want is:

_____
_____
_____
_____
_____
_____
_____
_____

# day 5

This needs to happen for the incompletion that
is most weighing down on me to be resolved:

_____

_____

_____

_____

_____

_____

_____

_____

_____

The specific action or practice I will do to resolve or complete it is:

_____

_____

_____

_____

_____

_____

_____

# day 6

This is what I need to know or do in order to complete my incompletion:

_____

_____

_____

_____

_____

_____

_____

_____

_____

_____

_____

_____

The specific date I will have it resolved or completed is:

_____ / _____ / _____

# day 7: *end-of-week reflections*

## My Experience of Calibration

**This is what I experienced when calibrating over the last week:**

_____
_____
_____
_____
_____
_____
_____
_____
_____
_____

I was surprised by:

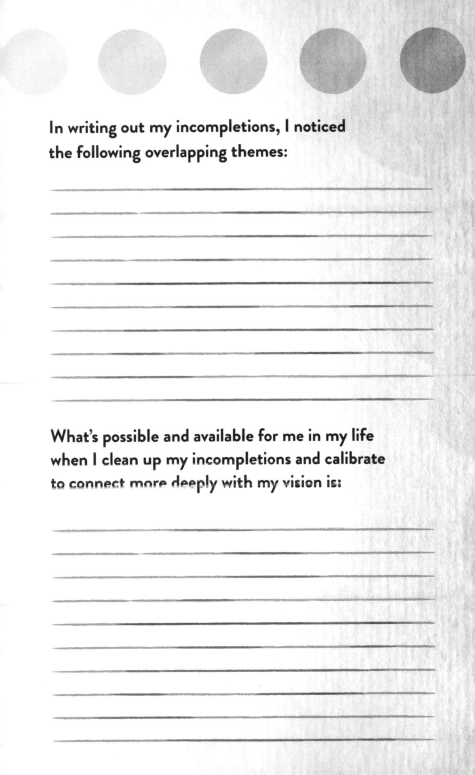

In writing out my incompletions, I noticed the following overlapping themes:

_____

_____

_____

_____

_____

_____

_____

_____

What's possible and available for me in my life when I clean up my incompletions and calibrate to connect more deeply with my vision is:

_____

_____

_____

_____

_____

_____

_____

_____

# self-honoring & non-negotiables

I will do this to connect with myself in the morning:

I will do this to connect with myself in the evening:

*Now, identify one specific action you're willing to commit to this week. It might be something you are eliminating or adding to your life. It should be something specific you're committing to and willing to be held accountable for.*

**One action I am choosing
to take now to honor myself
and reinvent my life is:**

**I acknowledge myself for:**

WEEK 3

# Beliefs

*I'm not good enough. I'm just not enough, period. There must be
something wrong with me. I'm not lovable.*

Do any of the above stories sound familiar to you? They tend to
lurk in the corners of our awareness—ready to pounce at the slightest
possibility of change. Sometimes, they can crop up so subtly that
they're hard to spot.

Our choices and actions are driven by the stories we tell ourselves
about the world, about other people, and about ourselves. This week,
we'll be working with the stories that become the foundation of our
beliefs. A belief is simply a long-held idea about the way the world
works, and our role within it. Even when we haven't explicitly identified
our beliefs, they are there in the background, informing every choice
we make, as well as what we do or don't do in service of our vision.

We're looking more closely at our beliefs this week because, even
though we might think we already know what they are, the truth is
that we tend to take our beliefs for granted until they become virtu-
ally imperceptible to us. The great thing is, our beliefs become evident
through our actions—and in the last two weeks, you've probably come

face to face with some of your beliefs without even realizing it! In fact, sometimes we only start to realize the beliefs that are operating in our lives when we encounter resistance, setbacks, or inertia—which is when we can ask ourselves: *What am I making this experience mean? What belief does that translate to?*

When it comes to reinventing yourself or your life, you will undoubtedly encounter stories you've internalized about yourself, others, and the world around you. It's time to start paying attention to these stories! How often have you resigned yourself to "this is just the way it is"? How many times have you imagined reinventing yourself, only to be overcome seconds later with a series of stories that serve to convince you that change is impossible?

Here's what some of these stories might sound like:

- *I'm too old (or I'm too young).*

- *It's too hard to change.*

- *I have no time to focus on transformation—I'm too busy with* [fill in the blank with your favorite excuse].

- *It won't work.*

- *My family will reject me if I change too much.*

- *I'm too rigid and stubborn.*

- *People rely on me, so I can't afford to reinvent myself.*

Here's the thing: Beliefs are just stories we tell ourselves—and very likely, stories we've been telling ourselves for such a long time that they can deceive us by appearing true. That's because they look a whole lot like facts based on empirical evidence that we ourselves have collected over the years! They're absolute. They're firm. And we've seen them proved "right" countless times throughout our lives. They even *feel* like facts. But the truth is, if we were to test these so-called facts with a simple inquiry, we'd see just how faulty they are.

# Changing Your Beliefs Is an Inside Job

A belief is something we think is true—even though that may not be the case. (Let's not forget: People thought the sun and planets revolved around Earth, and they were convinced that Earth was flat.) Once we update our operating software in the way that we discussed during our week of Calibration, it becomes easier to question and amend outdated beliefs.

Just to be clear, I'm not saying that all our beliefs are "bad." In fact, when it comes to the beliefs we harbor that hold us back from making the changes that would move us closer to our vision, even they have a purpose! Here's what's so incredible—your unconscious mind is actually bringing forth these stories as a way to protect you from getting hurt. Your unconscious mind collects a number of limiting beliefs (also called shadow beliefs because they tend to hang out in the dark, where they remain undetected) that hold you back from taking the action you want to take—without your even knowing! Yup, the unconscious mind is a sneaky genius.

We may have forgotten ever forming our limiting beliefs in the first place, but somewhere along the way, we began to operate as if our beliefs were just the facts of life. These beliefs have tremendous influence over our lives, telling us what we can and cannot do—and this begins at a tender young age. When we're under the age of 10, we're unable to process and digest our most significant experiences, or contextualize them in a broader way. This is precisely why we make everything mean something about us when we're young. We don't have the cognitive bandwidth to take in everything that's going on, and we're still pretty self-centered on top of that. If our mother is yelling at us, instead of drawing the conclusion that *Mom had a crummy day, and she's upset about something*, we personalize the whole thing into *Mom is mad at me, so I must be bad*. At a young age, this is the only way we can make sense of troublesome external circumstances—in relationship to us!

We draw conclusions about ourselves based on these experiences, and they become embedded as beliefs. Sure, some of those beliefs might suck the hope and vitality out of us, but remember, they also function as a protective mechanism because they keep us from taking any major risks that could elevate us to the next level in our lives. We might be miserable and our self-esteem could be taking a beating, but at least we're safe, right?

Our shadow beliefs ultimately funnel into the singular belief of *I'm not worthy. I'm not worthy of love. I'm not worthy of joy. I'm not worthy of safety. I'm not worthy of happiness. I'm not worthy of money.*

When we feel unworthy, we doubt our sense of *enoughness*, which means we tamp down on our desires, which means we continue to hold back from our most fulfilling vision. Simply put, our limiting beliefs tend to immobilize us, which isn't exactly conducive to taking action!

Intellectually, we might know that we, like every other being on this planet, are worthy of living the life of our dreams. We *know* that the negative or self-defeating thoughts that cross our mind can't be true—but that doesn't really matter if our unconscious mind has absorbed them and is acting out in ways that reinforce our old stories.

If any of what I've said resonates or sounds familiar to you, I invite you to be very compassionate with yourself. At the same time, it's essential to understand that although we are just protecting ourselves from plausible disappointment and hurt, *our beliefs are magnetic*. We draw the relationships, situations, and circumstances into our lives that reinforce what we already believe. Limiting beliefs act like a tractor beam, pulling into our lives the exact people and experiences that will mirror the belief and prove it right. So, if any of those relationships, situations, and circumstances are sources of worry and pain, I urge you to look at some of the beliefs you're holding that are making those things possible! (Spoiler alert: That's exactly what we'll be working on this week!)

Let's recap. This is how limiting/shadow beliefs form: Something happens when you're young. You make it mean something about you. You tell yourself a story based on the conclusion you've drawn. Then your story gets buried in your unconscious—only to surface whenever you're about to push the edge of your personal comfort zone. When you're actually primed to enter the next phase of your growth, that shadow sneaks up on you—filling you with self-doubt and millions of reasons not to do the thing you'd set out to do.

These limiting beliefs are so powerful because they become the lens we look through when we evaluate ourselves and our capacity for change. We're so attached to being *right* that we go through life collecting evidence of just how right we are about our limitations—until our limitations become all we can see!

The thing is, although you may have been indoctrinated with specific beliefs (by family, peers, and society at large), nobody else can really change your belief system. It's an inside job, meaning *you* have to do that for yourself. It begins by separating the wheat from the chaff . . . by looking at the beliefs you've unwittingly inherited, and deciding which ones get to stay because they are serving you and which ones need to be tossed into the trash because they are hindering your progress and keeping you from your best life.

Let's take a simple example. Maybe you're someone who tells yourself that you've invested so much in your career—time, money, education, etc.—and you can't switch careers or industries, otherwise all that effort will be wasted. Or perhaps you feel this way about a relationship in which you've invested a whole lot—which translates to your belief that you can't just leave . . . and if you do, you're a failure.

Is this factually true, or is it a belief? A story you tell yourself that may be the result of the meaning you created around a similar situation that happened very long ago?

Our pain stems from the story we wrap around the facts. Unless we learn how to separate fact from fiction, we'll stay rooted in our beliefs and unable to move

**It's essential to be open to possibility if you truly want to reinvent yourself or your life.**

forward. Staying stuck in disempowering beliefs keeps us from seeing solutions or options—and it's essential to be open to possibility if you truly want to reinvent yourself or your life.

While it's natural to default to the negative, it becomes a self-fulfilling prophecy, since science has proven there's a negative bias in the brain. The negative bias is a hardwired tendency to register negative experiences more easily and readily than positive ones—and to dwell on them, even years later and in excruciatingly vivid detail! This is why negative first impressions can stick with us for so long, and why we feel the pain and indignity of an insult or offhand remark more acutely than we do the sweetness of praise and compliments.

In other words, if we look for what's wrong, we'll find it.

The good news is, you don't have to cling to the stories you've been believing. You can choose to build your belief muscle in the other direction and lean into the positive by looking for what's right. The grown-up version of you now gets to step in and consciously install a new, empowering, supportive belief into your operating system so you can resume your process of reinvention.

Here's how a positive belief that counters the limiting belief might look. Let's work with that earlier example I offered: You've invested too much in your relationship to leave. And if you leave, it would be a waste of all that effort—on top of that, it would mean you're a failure.

Let's unpack some of the beliefs that underpin this particular story, because there are a few of them floating around here:

- *A successful relationship is one that has longevity.*

- *If something doesn't work out, the effort I put into it is completely wasted.*

- *If something doesn't work out, it means I've failed.*

If we take the time to examine each of these beliefs, we'll quickly see they don't hold up. Let's break each one down:

- *A successful relationship is one that has longevity.* The idea that two people should remain in a relationship even when they've shifted significantly over the years is so yesterday. Plenty of relationships change over time. That doesn't discount the fact that there were good times and valuable lessons. It doesn't negate the love that was there; in some cases, the love doesn't disappear at all—the only thing that changes is the idea that the relationship should continue, even when it's no longer working for both partners.

- *If something doesn't work out, the effort I put into it is completely wasted.* When someone invests in a relationship, those efforts don't just fly out the window; they have the potential to lead to valuable lessons and new understandings—like the idea that a relationship isn't just about "work." It should also be fun and rewarding. These insights will serve us in other areas of our life, as well as future relationships.

- *If something doesn't work out, it means I've failed.* The pop star Rihanna has a tattoo that says, "Never a failure, always a lesson." Often, our so-called failures become the foundation for our future successes because they teach us important lessons about who we are and what we want—which means they bring us even closer to our vision.

Allow this to take root inside of you: *The only thing keeping your limiting belief alive is that you believe it.* Give yourself the opportunity to consciously create a new belief to replace the old one—because whatever the old belief is, it was not consciously created. You're all grown up now. You're incredibly resilient, and you've built a lifetime of skills to help you get to where you need to go. Don't let some false story stand in your way. You get to consciously create a new belief to replace the old one! Isn't that exciting?

> **The only thing keeping your limiting belief alive is that you believe it.**

Let's look at some new beliefs to replace the old ones from the example above.

- *A successful relationship is one that has longevity* becomes *A successful relationship is one in which I've given it my best and I've learned a lot of lessons in the process.*

- *If something doesn't work out, the effort I put into it is completely wasted* becomes *No efforts are wasted when they come from a place of love and care.*

- *If something doesn't work out, it means I've failed* becomes *I can never fail—I can only produce results, which offer me valuable information about where to go next.*

Sometimes, the new belief can literally be the limiting belief shifted into its opposite. Or it might need different language that shifts your focus to empowering, positive actions you can take. Allow yourself to access a new belief to support your choices, actions, and process of reinvention. Remember, everything we do, every choice, every action, is either going to serve or sabotage, and what we believe about ourselves is one of the foremost and fundamental ways we sabotage ourselves.

Just as the process of calibration that you went through last week was strength training in the movement of greater adaptability, addressing and changing your limiting beliefs is an exercise in mental resculpting. In much the same way that athletes might sculpt their bodies through continual exertion, shifting your beliefs is all about eliminating excessive or unwanted stories and shaping your inner world in a way that actually benefits you.

It isn't enough to speak your new belief into existence. This is where you must supplement your new belief with action. New habits and behaviors literally carve out new neural pathways in your brain; the "grooves" in these pathways become deeper and more pronounced through repetition of these new behaviors. In other words, declaring your new belief as a positive affirmation is totally fine, but this positive belief is only as meaningful as the action you take to support it! This is how you're going to anchor in that new belief so it sticks around long term—and so that you easily default to the new belief, not to the same old sabotaging, limiting shadow belief.

May you take this week to recognize all the amazing, powerful things that are possible and available to you when you commit to living in alignment with your new belief!

# day 1

*Identify a current circumstance or situation in your life that has you feeling dissatisfied, stuck, frustrated, or blocked.*

**In the presence of this circumstance or situation, what story do you tell yourself about why your life is this way?**

_____

_____

_____

_____

_____

_____

_____

_____

_____

**What is the limiting belief
holding this particular story in place?**
(It might sound like this: "The story I tell
myself is _____ because I am _____," or
"The story I tell myself is _____ because I am not _____.")

_____

_____

_____

_____

_____

# day 2

*In the presence of your limiting belief, allow any memories to surface, from under the age of 10, that had you draw this conclusion about yourself and form this belief. If no memories come to you, notice if your body is trying to tell you anything.*

**Write down whatever arises.**

_____

_____

_____

_____

_____

_____

_____

_____

_____

_____

_____

_____

_____

# day 3

Identify a time in your life that this belief was proven untrue, in any context. (*If you're struggling to find a time in the past, let yourself imagine a scenario in your life where this belief could be proven untrue.*)

The story I tell myself is:

_____

_____

_____

_____

_____

_____

_____

_____

_____

_____

This is how it gets in the way:

# day 4

*Take a moment to notice how the stories you believe about yourself, or who you need to be, are in the way of fulfilling your vision.*

_____

_____

_____

_____

_____

_____

_____

_____

_____

_____

_____

_____

_____

_____

# day 5

In the spirit of elimination, think about what you can do to release the old belief. Maybe you can write it down on a piece of paper and burn it. Or make a list of even more times it's been proven untrue.

What action can you take to let go of this old belief?

# day 6

**What new belief can you consciously create to replace the old one?**

_____
_____
_____
_____
_____
_____
_____
_____
_____
_____
_____

What action can you take to cement this belief?

# day 7: *end-of-week reflections*

## My Experience of Beliefs

**This is what I experienced when exploring my beliefs over the last week:**

_____
_____
_____
_____
_____
_____
_____
_____
_____

I was surprised by:

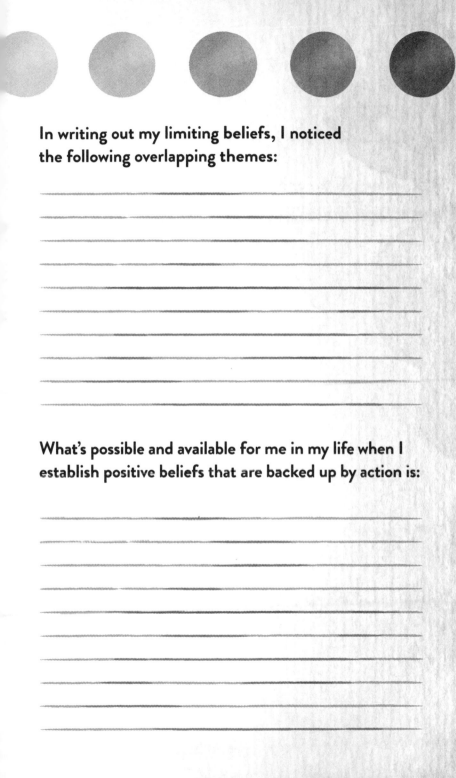

**In writing out my limiting beliefs, I noticed the following overlapping themes:**

_____

_____

_____

_____

_____

_____

_____

_____

_____

_____

**What's possible and available for me in my life when I establish positive beliefs that are backed up by action is:**

_____

_____

_____

_____

_____

_____

_____

_____

_____

_____

# self-honoring & non-negotiables

I will do this to connect with
myself in the morning:

I will do this to connect with
myself in the evening:

*Now, identify one specific action you're willing to commit to this week. It might be something you are eliminating or adding to your life. It should be something specific you're committing to and willing to be held accountable for.*

**One action I am choosing
to take now to honor myself
and reinvent my life is:**

**I acknowledge myself for:**

# Self-Worth

This week, we're exploring self-worth—something that is so vital to our well-being but that most of us have gotten all backward! Our feelings of self-worth tend to revolve around desirable outcomes in our world (that is, *If I get that job or lose those pounds, I'll finally feel worthy*). However, self-worth is not something that a person or shifting external circumstance can ever confer upon us. Self-worth is the acceptance and celebration of our wholeness, so we are no longer driven to trade parts of ourselves for validation, approval, and love. From this deep, unwavering belief in our inherent worth, we can cultivate the kind of mindset that helps us move mountains—not through effort or a zeal for productivity, but from a place of genuine joy that doesn't get deterred by "setbacks."

Worthiness is an inside job. It begins from within, and then we magnetize toward us that which reflects our inner sense of our own worthiness. So, we need to work with our own inner world in order to be the magnet that draws toward us what we are already worthy of. It's an elegant and easeful formula: In order to live out our vision, we have to know and believe we are inherently worthy. When we operate from inherent self-worth, moving toward our vision becomes a beautiful adventure to enjoy rather than a to-do list of items to check off. What we attain along the way—be it love, money, creative freedom, or anything else we've set our sights on—is the cherry on top, not the reason for setting out to begin with.

Notice that I mentioned the necessity of a "deep, unwavering belief in our inherent worth." You've probably suspected by now that our beliefs are constantly informing us about our level of self-worth. As we explored last week, most of us are operating on the shadow belief that we are unworthy, that we are severely lacking in some important quality, which is why we keep trying to fill that void with external achievements. We are mostly taught that we have to prove or earn our self-worth. We hitch our worthiness to someone else's wagon, which puts us in a precarious position of allowing someone else to determine our worth. However, if we're constantly waiting for something outside of us to deem us worthy, we will always find reasons for why our efforts are "not enough" or how they could be "even better." Our typical definitions of "success" are part of a constantly moving target. We tend to raise the bar on our expectations as soon as we meet them: If we lose 10 pounds we wonder what would happen if we lost 20. If we notice that someone else has something we don't, we get caught in the trap of comparison and start judging ourselves. Although it's great to reassess our goals, our dissatisfaction with what we've already accomplished and the need to do "better" is an insidious way we keep ourselves from feeling worthy.

Practicing the art of change isn't about getting stuck in the hamster wheel of "never enough"! It's about creating and moving toward a vision that reconnects you to your essence. What's more, your ability

**In order to live out our vision, we have to know and believe we are inherently worthy.**

60

> **Your ability to have the life you want is directly correlated with your ability to own your self-worth.**

to have the life you want is directly correlated with your ability to own your self-worth. An essential dimension of reinvention is valuing yourself *without conditions*. Without chasing approval or validation.

*To move forward with reinvention, we need to believe and trust that we are worthy, simply by being who we are. There is nothing we have to do, earn, or prove in order to be worthy.*

When we operate from a sense of our inherent worth, we develop an internal stability that is not rocked or taken off the rails by something outside of us. This gives us the power and momentum to keep moving in the direction of our authentic vision, even if we get thrown off now and then. We give ourselves permission to feel our full worthiness here and now—not on the basis of some future milestone. We no longer place conditions on our worth. We get to love ourselves just as we are, period!

One of the tools we can always depend on to increase our self-worth is a heaping dose of healthy selfishness—whose benefits we already discussed in our first week, when we focused on cultivating a powerful vision for our lives. Most of us spend all our time running around taking actions for *other* people, which doesn't help us create the change we most desire. But here's the deal: Selfishness is the foundation for a great life. I'm talking about the kind of selfishness that fills your cup and allows you to ditch your people-pleasing ways so you can get your *own* needs met. Remember, when you learn to make yourself, and your needs, a priority, you have a greater ability to be there for others in a more caring, genuine way. You learn that selfishness, self-care, and self-love are three sisters whose job it is to

> **Selfishness, self-care, and self-love are three sisters whose job it is to support you in honoring yourself.**

support you in honoring yourself. And all three of these qualities enable you to place much-needed attention on yourself, which is how you begin to reclaim the lost pieces of who you are and move into change with greater confidence.

## Reclaiming Wholeness

Most of us believe we have to hide some part of ourselves in order to be loved and accepted—in order to be worthy. These are the parts we don't want anyone to see—that we don't even want to *be*. While we may think we want to be loved for all of who we are, we actually expend tremendous energy on hiding.

The art of change is predicated on the concept of our wholeness. Paradoxically, rather than attempting to change who we essentially are, we are removing the obstacles that get in the way of recognizing that *we already are everything*. Every quality, every characteristic that exists in the universe, that we see in others, exists within us. It is when we claim our wholeness and remove the obstacles that stand in the way of it that we discover our endless capacity for reinvention.

While we are already whole, there are many parts of us that remain dormant. Let me offer an analogy to show you what I mean: We know the moon is always there, revolving around Earth, but we see it in different phases. When it's fully illuminated by the sun, it appears as a perfect round ball. But when the moon is waxing or waning, we only see parts of it, while other parts remain immersed in darkness. However, the moon is always whole, no matter what we do or don't see. It is simply revealing or concealing itself at different times. We do the same thing in that we spend a good chunk of our lives concealing parts of ourselves that we don't want others to see. While this never takes away from our wholeness, our willingness to activate and embrace those dormant parts of who we are is one of the biggest ways we can claim our inherent self-worth. Because if we recognize our wholeness, we are no longer afraid to step up and express even more of it—which is exactly how we move toward greater authenticity.

Of course, all of this is easier said than done. Growing up, we receive plenty of messages about what *not* to be. Your parents might have told you, "Don't be lazy" or "Don't be greedy." Perhaps you overheard a conversation in which they were judging a family down the street. Maybe you watched someone get bullied for being different or you witnessed a teacher shame a student struggling in school for being stupid.

When this happens, we decide, *I don't want to be that!* and we reject entire parts of ourselves, stuffing down those qualities in order to be acceptable, safe, loved, and lovable. As we go through life, we judge parts of ourselves as "right" or "wrong," "good" or "bad," based on the messages we've received from our parents, our caregivers, institutions like schools and places of worship, and the culture as

Every quality, every characteristic that exists in the universe, that we see in others, exists within us. It is when we claim our wholeness and remove the obstacles that stand in the way of it that we discover our endless capacity for reinvention.

a whole. We continue to reject the qualities in ourselves we have deemed wrong or distasteful. Then, we overcompensate to prove we're *not that*. If we don't want to be stupid, we may accrue many advanced degrees to prove our intelligence. If we don't want to be needy, we might never ask for help. Conversely, depending on how we were raised, we might even reject some qualities that could be considered positive by others; for example, maybe we were taught that displaying confidence makes us vulnerable to other people's judgments. In this way, we might have a skewed perception of normally positive traits that can impact the way we move through the world. (More about this when we get to the week of Visibility!)

**We reject entire parts of ourselves, stuffing down those qualities in order to be acceptable, safe, loved, and lovable.**

Can you see how this works? Any particular qualities coming to mind that you're aware of rejecting?

The most effective way to find the qualities we've rejected in ourselves is to see them in others. Whatever we don't own about ourselves, we project onto other people. In other words, you'll find your disowned qualities when you're triggered by these qualities in someone else. The great thing is, we will always have plenty of opportunities to claim our wholeness because life will constantly reveal our triggers! For example, if you have absolutely rejected the quality of selfishness, who will you attract into your life? Selfish people. The more you disown laziness, the more you'll be irritated by all the lazy people around you. What you resist persists! And it doesn't melt away until you detach from those projections and own them as part of you, and part of your wholeness.

You might be thinking, *How can it be that owning negative qualities in myself can do anything good for my sense of self-worth? That's crazy!* Let's use another analogy. Imagine having a hundred different electrical outlets on your chest. Each outlet represents a different quality or characteristic. The qualities we acknowledge and embrace in ourselves have cover plates over them. They are safe, as no electricity runs through them. But the qualities we're not okay with, which we have not yet owned in ourselves, have a charge. So when others come along and act out one of these qualities, they plug right into us and we get triggered. For example, if we deny or are uncomfortable with our anger, we will continually attract angry people into our lives. We will suppress our own angry feelings and judge people we see as angry.

One of the ways we avoid owning up to possessing a certain quality we see in someone else is by saying, "I'm not that because I don't do [fill in the blank with the behavior that's connected to your 'favorite' trigger]." When looking for these qualities within ourselves, it's important to note that we may not exhibit or express them the same way someone else does. We're looking for the deeper quality beneath the behavior. It's essential to discover the way the quality is present in our own behaviors and attitudes, so we can reclaim it and therefore diffuse the charge.

Here's how this works: Think for a moment about someone close to you. Take a moment to mentally identify the behavior that triggers you (e.g., someone is dismissive to waitstaff and people in customer service), and then identify the quality beneath the behavior (e.g., bitchiness). Now, ask yourself, "How do I express this same quality?" Maybe your "bitchiness" doesn't come across in interactions with store clerks or waiters, but in the condescending tone you use with your partner or children. Now, ask yourself, "How do I overcompensate for the rejection of this quality?" Maybe you realize that you overcompensate by being overly polite and fixating on "good" manners. See if you can accept your disowned quality. Try it on right now. Say, "I am bitchy." Not easy, but the truth is, we can all be bitchy from time to time. That's just a tiny part of who we are, but a part all the same. Embrace this quality and recognize the gift it offers you.

After all, being bitchy from time to time is sometimes necessary, like in situations when we need to stand up for ourselves.

Let's look at another quality. For example, maybe you're triggered by a sibling's tendency to never finish what they start. Maybe you're triggered by this behavior because it points to the underlying quality of laziness. This indicates that you've disowned your laziness. You need to reclaim and integrate it so that you're no longer triggered. You don't have a problem finishing what you start, but you acknowledge that your laziness presents as binge-watching your favorite show in the middle of the day. However, you've overcompensated for your laziness your entire life by hiding it under the guise of being an overachiever. Saying "I am lazy" stings at first, but you learn to embrace the not-so-obvious gifts of laziness—such as the fact that it allows you to rest, rejuvenate, replenish, and enjoy life.

Hopefully, you can already see the value of owning and embracing the qualities you've rejected within yourself; when you do this, you'll discover that you're no longer drawing people with these qualities toward you, and you aren't triggered when others display these qualities. Also, by integrating these qualities, you no longer feel the need to define your self-worth on the basis of upholding a narrow selection of qualities that elicit your desired outcomes in the world. You recognize that you can love yourself here and now, for *all* of who you are. You increase your self-worth effortlessly as you welcome your wholeness, which enables you to become even more of who you are and to shine your radiant light in the world!

I know it can be challenging to imagine owning and embracing parts of yourself you've judged as bad and wrong for so long. I promise you, though, that every part of you comes bearing gifts. Think about it: When could it come in handy to be bitchy? When would it be useful to be lazy? We often keep these parts of ourselves locked away because we think that if we accept them, they'll run amok. But that's not actually how it works. When you consciously own and embrace a quality, you regain access to it. It becomes available as a tool in your tool kit that you can choose to use, if and when it serves you. It's only when we keep these parts of ourselves locked away and hidden that they come out sideways. The qualities themselves are charge-neutral; we're the ones who puts the positive or negative spin on them.

The process of reinvention is designed to support you in returning to your essence, to wholeness, to the full truth of who you are. It's time to reclaim the lost pieces of you, to own and embrace all that you are, so you can live the life you are truly worthy of!

# day 1

**The ways I try to prove my value or earn my worth—at home, at work, with family, with friends—are:**

_____

_____

_____

_____

_____

_____

_____

_____

_____

_____

_____

_____

_____

_____

_____

_____

_____

_____

# day 2

The earliest messages I remember receiving that have informed my sense of self-worth are:

_____

_____

_____

_____

_____

_____

The ways these messages are informing my life today are:

_____

_____

_____

_____

_____

_____

_____

_____

# day 3

The qualities or characteristics I most don't want to be, or be called (e.g., needy, lazy, greedy, irresponsible, mean, etc.), are:

_____

_____

_____

_____

_____

_____

_____

_____

The ways I overcompensate for and hide the qualities I don't want to be, in order to prove I'm *not* that, are:

_____

_____

_____

_____

_____

_____

_____

_____

# day 4

Reflecting on the qualities I don't want to be that I wrote down yesterday, the quality that stings the most is:

_____

_____

_____

_____

The person who most reflects this quality back to me is:

rejected that quality the following age and for this reason:

A time in my life when I have expressed this quality is:

# day 5

Reflecting on the quality I wrote about yesterday, the gifts this quality brings me are:

_____

_____

_____

_____

_____

_____

_____

_____

The action I'm taking this week to own and embrace this quality is:

_____

_____

_____

_____

_____

_____

_____

_____

_____

# day 6

What I need to release in order to feel worthy of
bringing my vision to fruition is:

_____

_____

_____

_____

_____

_____

_____

_____

What I need to know in order to reclaim my wholeness
and fully stand in my self-worth is:

_____

_____

_____

_____

_____

_____

_____

# **day 7:** *end-of-week reflections*

## My Experience of Self-Worth

**This is what I experienced when exploring self-worth over the last week:**

_____

_____

_____

_____

_____

_____

_____

_____

_____

I was surprised by:

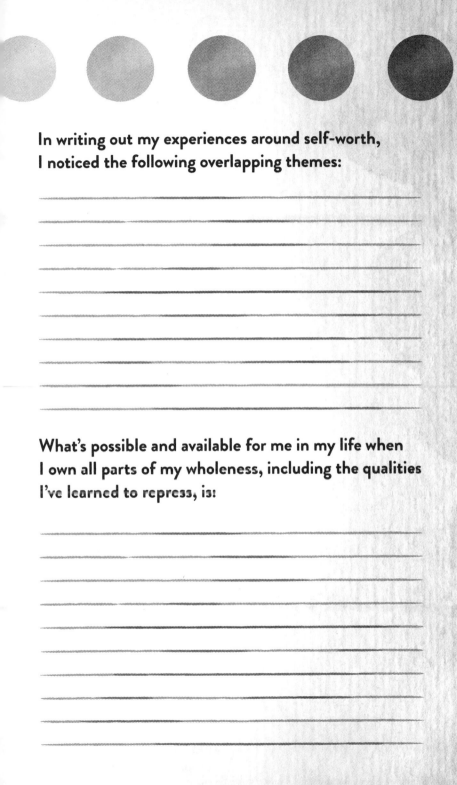

In writing out my experiences around self-worth,
I noticed the following overlapping themes:

_____

_____

_____

_____

_____

_____

_____

_____

_____

What's possible and available for me in my life when
I own all parts of my wholeness, including the qualities
I've learned to repress, is:

_____

_____

_____

_____

_____

_____

_____

_____

_____

_____

# self-honoring & non-negotiables

I will do this to connect with myself in the morning:

I will do this to connect with myself in the evening:

*Now, identify one specific action you're willing to commit to this week. It might be something you are eliminating or adding to your life. It should be something specific you're committing to and willing to be held accountable for.*

**One action I am choosing
to take now to honor myself
and reinvent my life is:**

**I acknowledge myself for:**

# Boundaries

This week, we're diving into one of my favorite topics: boundaries. Together, we'll explore the ins and outs of boundaries: what they are, what they are not, why they're essential, and how they're absolutely integral to the process of moving toward your vision and sustaining the art of change! You'll learn to discover and dissolve whatever stands in the way of making yourself a priority, and you'll also see how your boundaries become the scaffolding that holds each dimension of your reinvention in place.

Just so we're on the same page, I'd like to offer the definition of boundaries that we'll be working with. Boundaries are the limits that you set to define what you will and will not do, and what you will or will not accept or tolerate.

Before we get in too deep, let's take a look at some beliefs and excuses that are fairly common around setting and maintaining boundaries, and that contribute to our resistance in doing so. They include:

- *Boundaries are hard to set and keep.*
- *Boundaries limit my options and close me off to new possibilities.*

- *Boundaries are selfish.*
- *Boundaries cause conflict.*
- *If I set a boundary, I will lose everything.*
- *If I set a boundary, no one will like me and I'll be abandoned.*

The truth is, our own beliefs and excuses around boundaries are what keep us from setting and maintaining them. And make no mistake—when we don't hold boundaries, we are much more susceptible to being pulled out of our center. We lose our alignment with what's true for us. It's almost as if, by not staying grounded in our own lives, we become trespassers in other people's territories. We start mistaking our surroundings for our natural habitat—which is why it's so easy to lose sight of our vision when we don't have boundaries.

A lot of times, we develop an aversion to boundaries because it's common to think of them as restrictive and limiting. However, I invite you to see them as expansive. In truth, boundaries take us closer to our vision because they support us in affirming our authentic selves by carefully choosing and consciously curating the content of our lives. They help us to define what we value by creating a meaningful container for our vision. They help us to inhabit our lives with more purpose and greater fidelity to our vision.

When we do not honor our own boundaries, this is usually because we've packaged ourselves to be digestible to others. After all, most of us are trained to fit into the mold of who others want us to be. Let me give you an example. Imagine you're going on a first date. What are the tiny ways you might find yourself crossing your own boundaries in order to be liked by the other person? This can be as simple as laughing at jokes you don't actually find funny, or sharing a dish at a restaurant that includes food you don't like or might even be allergic to. All this, because you're trying to be something someone else wants you to be (or at least, the version you think will be palatable to them).

Sometimes, we are so eager to be picked and chosen by others that we forget freedom comes from being the one who gets to pick and choose! And this, my friend, is what I want you to consider: Setting boundaries allows you to pick and choose what you will and will not allow. Rather than being restrictive, boundaries give you agency and a sense of being centered in your truth. They are a major source of freedom! Boundaries are the trusty vehicle that helps you navigate the vast waters of your life's journey. And in order to practice the art of change, you need to make sure you're not traveling in a leaky boat.

Over the years, I've heard some version of the following: "I don't have a problem with setting boundaries! The problem is, people in my life are constantly testing and crossing my boundaries." But here's the kicker: *If your boundaries are being crossed, you're the one crossing them.* (You might want to read that last line a few times to really digest it!) It's not up to anyone else to respect, honor, or uphold them. Your boundaries are *yours* to set, as well as *yours* to maintain. Your boundaries are about *YOU*.

**If your boundaries are being crossed, you're the one crossing them.**

A boundary is *not* about wanting someone else to change. A boundary *is* about your own needs and what you will do to honor and care for yourself. Boundaries put you in the driver's seat. Boundaries help you clarify what's okay and not okay for you. Boundaries help you identify and express your needs.

Two major reasons people avoid setting boundaries are that they feel guilty doing so, or they fear the conflict that might arise as a result. But I have news for you: If you feel guilty when you set a boundary, that's good news! It means you're dissolving old patterns and finally honoring yourself. Most people think guilt is an indication that they shouldn't enforce a boundary, when in fact, it's a sign to keep going and to move forward with that boundary.

So, if you've ever felt guilty when you've done something positive for yourself that moves you closer to your vision, you can reframe it to mean that you are growing into the kind of person who is willing to stand in your desire, even if it makes you uncomfortable. Congratulations!

Now, let's look at conflict. What we seldom recognize is that the tendency to avoid external conflict only increases internal conflict. Most people try to avoid conflict because they don't want to disrupt the peace in a relationship. This is a surface-level attempt that often hides a deeper truth: What we fear isn't actually the conflict itself, but the possibility that the container of the relationship isn't strong enough to hold both our truth and the other person's. Instead of facing that possibility head on, we get into a toxic loop of doing or saying whatever we can to avoid ruffling any feathers. This attempt at "harmony" comes at a high cost, because it keeps us from authentically relating to others. And when we are not authentic, it's because we have not come into ownership of our wholeness, which is the very basis of self-worth.

Boundaries are meant to reinforce your self-worth. Boundaries give you the freedom and agency that are necessary components of the art of change. Boundaries ensure that your vision of reinvention becomes a reality.

**Boundaries ensure that your vision of reinvention becomes a reality.**

I'd even go so far as to say that what you don't have in your life is directly proportional to the boundaries you have *not* set. You pay a high price for not setting boundaries. These costs can include:

- Your unmet needs and desires
- Your lost time and energy
- Your silenced voice
- Honest, intimate relationships

- Hours committed to others' dreams at the expense of your own

- Feeling guilty, ashamed, less than, or resentful

Without boundaries to support you, you're likely tolerating the intolerable and accepting the unacceptable in some area of your life, if not several. If you remember the Calibration week, you probably also remember the importance of addressing incompletions. Crossing or failing to set meaningful boundaries is a specific type of incompletion that can derail us from our vision and create an invisible (or at least unexamined) obstacle that halts our momentum. In contrast, when we set and maintain boundaries, we develop a nurturing and loving relationship with ourselves that we need to stay aligned with our vision, and follow through with the choices and actions that connect us to reinvention each and every day.

Each time you set a healthy boundary, you're saying "Yes!" to you—reminding yourself that you are trustworthy and will follow through on your promise and commitment. This will move you out of blame and victim mode and into responsibility and empowerment. More importantly, it will steward you reliably in the direction of your vision.

## The Power of Putting Yourself First

When we set and maintain meaningful boundaries, we are essentially honoring our own limits—what is and is not acceptable for us. We are also respecting our own needs (for example, eight luxurious hours of sleep every night, or ample time with loved ones balanced by ample time in glorious solitude).

Are you willing to give yourself permission to consider your own needs *at least as much* as you are considering the needs of others? If your answer is yes, that's great . . . but I want to take it a step further. Are you willing to consider your own needs *more than* you are considering the needs of others? Here, you might be getting a little

> **Are you willing to give yourself permission to consider your own needs *at least as much* as you are considering the needs of others?**

uncomfortable, but stick with me. Are you willing to consider your own needs *first*—before you even start factoring anyone else into the equation?

That last suggestion might sound a little extreme at first glance, but you must consider your own needs first in order to set meaningful boundaries that help you maintain a sense of integrity and commitment to your vision. This is what leads to transformation. Now, it doesn't mean you are discounting anyone else's needs. It just means you're in the driver's seat of your life, filling the primary slot in your calendar.

I know this might sound easier said than done, especially because so many of us tend to put ourselves on the back burner or take ourselves off the agenda altogether! But the process of reinvention is about returning to our essence and becoming intimate with our authentic self. This requires knowing what's actually true for us—what we will and will not abide by. It requires moving past the fear of not being liked, displeasing others, being viewed as selfish, and all the excuses that intervene (and that sound so convincing when they do!) when we are tempted to abandon ourselves.

Let's look at a common way many people cross their own boundaries: by saying "yes" when they really want to say "no." A request comes in, and often, the first impulse that arises is a knee-jerk yes.

We don't necessarily slow down enough to acknowledge our reasons, but the underlying motivation is usually about avoiding conflict. We might be haunted by a lingering sense of obligation that was drummed into us at an early age. Or maybe we like fulfilling the role of rescuer, superhero, or fixer; maybe this identity gives us a sense of security or purpose, even though it doesn't actually serve us.

Again, all of the above reasons might *sound* convincing on the surface, but none of them point to a true and honest yes. The only reason to ever say "yes" is when something actually aligns with your desire. After all, desire is the basis of the vision you unearthed in Week 1, and it's the fuel that'll support you throughout your journey.

The antidote to the knee-jerk yes is to begin building in a pause before you respond to a request, so you can genuinely check in and ask yourself:

- *What do I think?*
- *What do I feel?*
- *What do I want?*
- *What do I need?*

The process of pausing and checking in is a good example of a boundary you set and maintain with yourself so you can easily respond with no, if you're ready to, or with, "I'll get back to you tomorrow," which is more genuine than an unthought-through yes.

The key to putting yourself first is to practice considering your own desires before you answer a request. With practice, the discomfort that surfaces when you pause and respond to the four questions above will melt away over time until checking in with yourself becomes second nature. If you discover that no is your honest response, remember that you can say "no" with gratitude and grace instead of excuses and apologies.

Of course, just as checking in with yourself requires practice, so does saying "no." You might feel uncomfortable saying no because you want to be seen a certain way, or you attach your worth to what you do for others. You might refrain from routinely making yourself a priority because there is no external validation in that. Maybe you don't take good care of yourself because there's no one giving you gold stars and celebrating your authenticity.

This is why one of the greatest opportunities you have throughout these eight weeks is to continuously locate yourself, focus on yourself, take your attention off of everyone else out there, and put it back on *you*. It's precisely why I guide you through the process of self-honoring at the end of each week—so you get into the habit of placing yourself at the center of your own life . . . so you really get to know who you are and what's important to you . . . so you have the self-awareness to calibrate and course-correct if needed.

I'm going to support you in keeping the focus on yourself by gently inviting you to return to *you* if you find your attention drifting to other people—what they want and need, how they're going to feel, what they're going to think, etc. You may have previously related this to being empathetic, giving, and loving. However, it's actually linked to living an *other-referenced* life, which means you center your life and needs around *other* people instead of making yourself the priority and respecting other people's right to act and react as they choose to.

**Boundaries support you in giving yourself permission to consider your own needs so you can show up for you, prioritize your preferences, and fulfill your desires.**

Boundaries support you in giving yourself permission to consider your own needs so you can show up for you, prioritize your preferences, and fulfill your desires. Amazingly, despite the fear of being seen as selfish or unkind, this can lead to greater intimacy and better, more authentic relationships. Think about it:

By choosing to verbalize and express a boundary, you are essentially giving others a page out of your operating manual—a piece of your puzzle, so to speak. It makes you more trustworthy, because if you're willing to be honest about your no, others will recognize they can wholeheartedly trust your yes. If you refrain from such honesty, what is your intimacy with others truly based on?

While setting and maintaining your boundaries can certainly bring about more fulfilling relationships, I want to bring the focus back to you. Your boundaries strengthen the relationship with the most important person of all: *YOU*. Your boundaries are the scaffolding that supports you in upholding your commitment to yourself and your vision—the choices you say you will make and the actions you say you will take—in service of your reinvention.

As you reconnect with yourself and come to understand who you truly are, boundaries will become a natural expression of protecting and growing the seed of desire within you. And before you know it, setting boundaries will become a way of life that you happily embrace.

# day 1

**The beliefs and excuses that are keeping me from setting and maintaining boundaries are:**

_____

_____

_____

_____

_____

_____

_____

_____

_____

_____

_____

_____

_____

_____

_____

_____

_____

_____

# day 2

What I know I want in my life but don't have yet is:

_____
_____
_____
_____
_____
_____
_____

The ways I'm preventing myself from having what I want are:

_____
_____
_____
_____
_____
_____
_____
_____
_____
_____

# day 3

What I will never again tolerate in my life is:

_____

_____

_____

_____

_____

_____

_____

_____

_____

_____

_____

# day 4

Here are some boundaries I can strengthen in the following specific areas:

- Health (Physical/Mental/Emotional):


- Creativity:


- Relationships:


- Career:


- Money:


- Adventure/Pleasure:


- Other:

# day 5

I do this even though I don't want to, and it weighs me down:

_____
_____
_____
_____
_____
_____
_____

I don't do this, even though it enlivens me and reminds me of who I am:

_____
_____
_____
_____
_____
_____
_____
_____

# day 6

Here's one thing
I know I want more of:

Here's one
thing
I know I want less of:

I choose to set this
boundary in order to
get more of what I want:

I choose to set this boundary in order to get less of
what I don't want:

# day 7: *end-of-week reflections*

## My Experience of Boundaries

**This is what I experienced when exploring boundaries over the last week:**

_____
_____
_____
_____
_____
_____
_____
_____
_____
_____

I was surprised by:

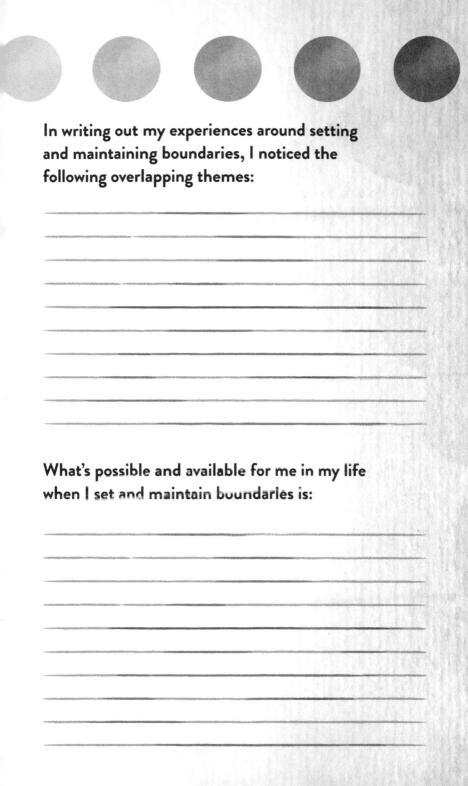

In writing out my experiences around setting and maintaining boundaries, I noticed the following overlapping themes:

_____

_____

_____

_____

_____

_____

_____

_____

_____

What's possible and available for me in my life when I set and maintain boundaries is:

_____

_____

_____

_____

_____

_____

_____

_____

_____

# self-honoring & non-negotiables

I will do this to connect with
myself in the morning:

I will do this to connect with
myself in the evening:

*Now, identify one specific action you're willing to commit to this week. It might be something you are eliminating or adding to your life. It should be something specific you're committing to and willing to be held accountable for.*

**One action I am choosing
to take now to honor myself
and reinvent my life is:**

**I acknowledge myself for:**

# Choice

This week, we'll be exploring the power of choice! Remember, choice is an integral part of the Transformation Equation we've previously talked about:

## Change = Vision + Choice + Action

When it comes to choice, it's all about connecting the cause and effect of our daily activities. Every single day is filled with a series of choices we make—some minor, some major. And every single one of these choices can impact our vision.

Every choice we've made up until this very moment has brought us here. If we don't make a different choice, our future arrives looking very much like our present and our past. And even if our present is great, the future can be even greater! So, this week, we're going to explore what it means to open up and expand our capacity to receive—and be receptive to even more.

There is a great power in being able to make different choices. Your present-moment choice is the crystal ball that predicts your future. We all want to know what the future holds, and the truth is, we

> **Your present-moment choice is the crystal ball that predicts your future.**

have tremendous power over our future based on the choices we make and the actions we take.

Every single choice we make does one of two things. It serves or sabotages our vision for our reinvention. That's it—one or the other. Every choice, every action, serves or sabotages, and we want to be taking the actions that serve and move us in the direction of our desire. Our choices and *non-choices* are dictated by our unconscious. When I talk about non-choices, in other words I mean the decisions we unwittingly make by simply *not* making a choice. Examples of non-choices can be:

- Procrastinating on writing that book we've been meaning to (a great example of an incompletion, which we explored during our Calibration week)

- Not deciding what we want to have for dinner and instead obliging our partner, who knows what they want (something that can set us up for a pattern of compliance, without our even knowing it!)

- Sticking with a job we don't really like because "it pays the bills" (even though there are any number of choices we can make to support both our security and our joy)

Even when we believe we don't have a choice, we forget the many ways in which we do—we forget that our agency extends to both the small and large stuff. If we choose not to make a choice, that *is* a choice! As I mentioned earlier, where we are in our lives is the culmination of all the choices we made, but it's also the culmination of all the choices we didn't make. We don't have ultimate control over everything that happens, but what we choose to do or not do creates a fertile ground for the outcomes we experience.

I can't count how many clients have shared with me some version of "I heard the voice in my head telling me not to walk down the aisle and I did, anyway." Often, the decision to ignore the voice of one's intuition comes from the fear of embarrassing oneself or disappointing someone else. However, the non-choice to ignore that voice, as well as the ensuing action, is what creates the circumstances that, 99 percent of the time, lead to the demise of such a marriage. This is because many of the aspects of our lives that negatively impact us can be traced back to a moment when we made the choice to cross our own boundaries and go against our better instincts.

Often, we're not even aware of the choices we're making or why we're making them. This is why it's so powerful to make conscious

**We're all completely capable of creating whatever it is we're most committed to; however, most people have *no idea* what it is they're *truly* most committed to. We all have underlying or hidden commitments that originated as promises we made to ourselves in childhood, usually as the result of a limiting belief.**

what is mostly unconscious. This is how we become awake and aware as we're making choices and taking actions.

As we awaken to the power of our choices, it's essential to be aware of our avoidance strategies, which might include eating, drinking, drugs, exercise, work, shopping, mindlessly surfing the Internet, scrolling, or watching TV. It's not that any of these avoidant strategies are *bad*, in and of themselves. It's about the way we use these strategies to go numb and avoid feeling or dealing. And in general, we resort to these activities unconsciously, meaning we give them power over our lives without even knowing it.

This week, choice is a demarcation point. We are moving into a place of conscious awareness and conscious choice. This week, you'll start to notice exactly how much your choices impact your world. Choice is a vital piece of the Transformation Equation, because there is a clear cause-and-effect relationship that shows us exactly how connected we are to our vision. Our choices impact the change we are making and the vision that we do (or don't) bring into fruition. And obviously, in order to take an action (the final piece of the equation) that brings us into greater alignment with our vision, we need to be willing to make a different choice.

Let's take mindless eating, for example. Considering your choice requires staying conscious and noticing you're going to the fridge right now. You're not even hungry, but you're going to the fridge. So, what is it you're choosing not to feel or deal with? Perhaps you just had a disturbing conversation with your partner, and it's too painful to sit with the implications of everything you discussed. Your willingness to acknowledge what's present is key. It allows you to pause for a moment to simply see what's here that you don't want to feel or deal with. Building in the pause increases conscious awareness so you don't go into autopilot mode. This is why it's so important to check in with your body—to really tune in to what you are feeling so you can begin to track the ways you're choosing to distract, avoid, or deny something.

At some point in our lives, many of us have felt stuck in place, unable to create the change we want. It can feel incredibly frustrating when you don't see movement! I don't want you to let this deter you, as it doesn't automatically mean you're not ready to reinvent yourself. Let me show you what might be at play.

## Understanding Our Deeper Commitments

Perhaps you've had the experience of setting a goal that you just can't seem to fulfill. Maybe the gap between what you want and what you actually have led to moments of feeling frustrated, disheartened, or self-doubting. If you can relate, you're not alone. What we think or say we're committed to is often at odds with a deeper commitment held in our unconscious mind. We believe we want one thing, but we're secretly committed to its opposite. The truth is, we're all completely capable of creating whatever it is we're most committed to; however, most people have no idea what it is they're truly most committed to.

We all have underlying or hidden commitments that originated as promises we made to ourselves in childhood, usually as the result of a limiting belief. Our hidden commitments are responses to our limiting beliefs. Hidden commitments are promises we made to ourselves to stay safe or feel loved. For example, perhaps we inherited an early limiting belief from our caregivers that only the most powerful and privileged among us get to enjoy life's pleasures. In order to belong to our family system, we might have developed a hidden commitment that says, "I'm committed to struggle." Perhaps another limiting belief that solidified at a young age was that expressing our authentic thoughts and feelings isn't acceptable

> **Hidden commitments are promises we made to ourselves to stay safe or feel loved.**

> **Whenever there is a discrepancy between what you say you want and what you're actually experiencing, it's a telltale sign that there's an old, outdated, underlying commitment in the mix that's keeping you from moving forward.**

and will gain us disapproval or even punishment. A resulting hidden commitment might have been, "I'm committed to not being too loud or opinionated." Such commitments explain the disconnect between what you say you want and what you actually experience. So whenever there is a discrepancy between what you say you want and what you're actually experiencing, it's a telltale sign that there's an old, outdated, underlying commitment in the mix that's keeping you from moving forward.

Consciously, you want to move toward the beautiful vision you've unearthed, but unconsciously, you are more in alignment with something *other than* what you are saying you want to be in alignment with. You're serving this hidden commitment instead of your vision and reinvention. Here are some other examples of authentic desires and the hidden commitments that lie beneath the surface.

- Desire: "I want to become a public speaker."

  Underlying commitment: "I am committed to staying small so that I won't be called stupid."

- Desire: "I want to start my own business."

  Underlying commitment: "I am committed to controlling everything so I feel safe, and having my own business feels very out of control."
- Desire: "I am going to be an artist."

  Underlying commitment: "I am committed to being an accountant because that's what my father was, and he died when I was young. I'll dishonor him if I do something else."

Are you starting to recognize the sneaky way underlying commitments secretly sabotage us?

If you've been feeling the impulse to reinvent yourself for some time but haven't been able to create real momentum, your underlying commitment has been holding you back. For example, let's say you want to start your own business, but your underlying commitment is to stay safe and small right where you are. Even as you make strides, some part of you is sabotaging those efforts and ensuring that you fail. Even though this might bring unhappiness and disappointment, it also gives that part of you that formed the commitment a sense of safety.

Underlying commitments cause us to take actions that lead us away from the direction of our dreams and paralyze us in patterns that we can't seem to change, no matter how hard we try.

Let's explore where these underlying commitments come from, and why they can be so challenging to budge.

When we were children, before our logical thinking minds were developed enough to process what was happening around us in a healthy way, we developed coping mechanisms and survival strategies to feel safe and loved. This is when we began packaging ourselves to be digestible to everyone else. We made promises to ourselves about ways to be in the world. Those promises got embedded deep in the recesses of our unconscious mind, but we are still loyal to them—even though we've long forgotten what they are.

Some examples of underlying commitments are:

- Staying silent
- Staying small
- Remaining invisible
- Not speaking your mind
- Not shining brighter than one of your siblings
- Not making as much money as your father
- Not drawing attention away from your mother
- Accepting struggle as a way of life
- Seeking comfort over growth

At first, underlying commitments will often show up as strategies around the way we're going to keep ourselves contained and stay out of trouble. Over time, these strategies become the seeds of the self-sabotage we experience as an adult. Once, I had a client who was a talented opera singer. She had no problem singing in private, but every time she went out on stage, she literally got stage fright and lost her voice. Through the work we did together, she was able to uncover and unpack an old, outdated commitment to staying silent—only being seen but not heard—which kept her safe as a child. Ultimately, she was able to go out onstage and sing, because she identified this old commitment and then made a new commitment to expressing herself and letting her voice be heard.

In the week ahead, you will uncover the primary hidden commitment you're still serving, and you will replace it with a new conscious, empowering commitment in alignment with what you actually want.

We can absolutely create anything that we are most committed to. I often call the instant this realization dawns on us as the "Dorothy moment," alluding to that scene in *The Wizard of Oz* where the good witch, Glinda, says to our heroine, "You've always had the power…" Just like Dorothy, we've had the power all along—it's just that our *commitment* has been misdirected. And the most powerful

106

choices we can make are the ones that realign us with our authentic desires and with the essence of who we are in the absence of fear or self-sabotage.

# day 1

*The first stage of this week's exploration is to expose the discrepancy between what you say you want and what you're actually experiencing. We'll begin with what you say you want. For example: "I say I want to save money to buy a house"; "I say I want to lose ten pounds"; or "I say I want a relationship." Select three things you say you want, and fill in the blanks below.*

I say I want:

I say I want:

I say I want:

# day 2

*Looking back at what you said you wanted in yesterday's prompt, identify the actions, habits, patterns, and choices that are inconsistent with what you say you want or that take you away from what you say you want. For example: "I say I want to save money to buy a house, but what I'm experiencing is late-night online shopping"; "I say I want to lose ten pounds, but what I'm experiencing is eating all the cookies"; or "I say I want a relationship, but what I'm experiencing is rejecting every dating opportunity that comes along." Using each of the three examples from yesterday, fill in the blanks below.*

I say I want

but what I'm
experiencing is

I say I want

but what I'm
experiencing is

I say I want

but what I'm
experiencing is

# day 3

*If the actions, habits, patterns, and choices you wrote down yesterday are inconsistent with what you say you want, they are directly reflecting back to you what you've secretly been most committed to. Remember, our outer world is a reflection of our inner commitments, so no matter what you are consciously telling yourself, what you're experiencing is revealing to you what you are actually committed to. Allow yourself to begin seeing the connection, the cause and effect. Write down your underlying commitments below. For example: "What I'm most committed to is immediate gratification"; "What I'm most committed to is being invisible"; or "What I'm most committed to is being alone." Build on the sentences you created yesterday to fill in the blanks below.*

I say I want _____
but what I'm experiencing is _____ ,
so what I'm most committed to is _____
_____ .

I say I want _____
but what I'm experiencing is _____ ,
so what I'm most committed to is _____
_____ .

I say I want _____
but what I'm experiencing is _____ ,
so what I'm most committed to is _____
_____ .

# day 4

*Choose the underlying commitment that is currently impacting your life the most. Connect back to the particular circumstance or situation in your life that had you make this commitment to yourself.*

**The underlying commitment currently impacting my life the most is:**

_____

_____

_____

_____

_____

_____

_____

**Where did this commitment originate?**
**What event, situation, or circumstance had me make this promise to myself?**
*(Note: it likely began when you were under 10 years old in your family of origin, with friends or at school.)*

_____

_____

_____

_____

_____

_____

_____

# day 5

*You now get to line up commitment and desire. Up until now in your life, they have been misaligned, and that is why you have not been able to have what you want. It has nothing to do with willpower or discipline. It has nothing to do with the way you've been consciously trying to get what you desire, because this has been happening on an unconscious level. It's time to take the attention off the old, outdated commitment that no longer serves you so you can insert a new commitment that is aligned with your desires into your operating system. (Remember, this commitment can be simple. It can be the opposite of the old one. It can be a commitment to be seen or heard. Just make sure it speaks to your authentic desires!) Fill in the blanks below.*

**My new conscious commitment is:**

**The thought, belief, or behavior I will need to eliminate, release, and give up in order to fully honor my new commitment is:**

# day 6

The action I will integrate in order to stay in alignment with my new commitment instead of regressing to the old, so I can move forward with momentum is:

_____

_____

_____

_____

_____

_____

_____

_____

_____

_____

# day 7: end-of-week reflections

## My Experience of Choice

**This is what I experienced when exploring choice over the last week:**

_____

_____

_____

_____

_____

_____

_____

_____

_____

_____

I was surprised by:

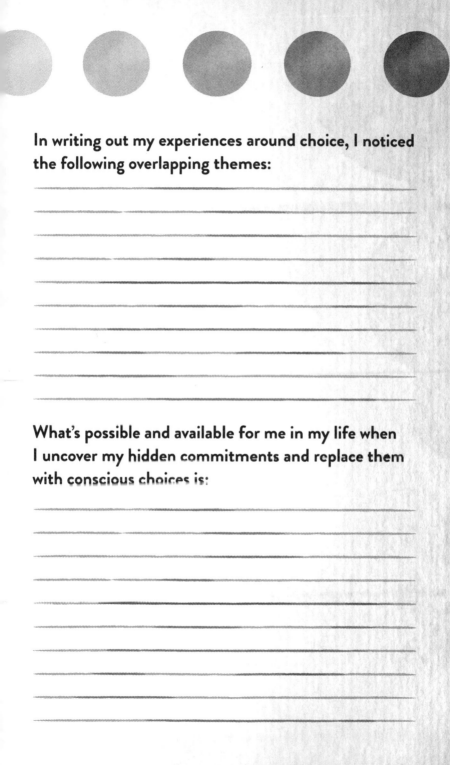

**In writing out my experiences around choice, I noticed the following overlapping themes:**

_____

_____

_____

_____

_____

_____

_____

_____

_____


**What's possible and available for me in my life when I uncover my hidden commitments and replace them with conscious choices is:**

_____

_____

_____

_____

_____

_____

_____

_____

_____

# self-honoring & non-negotiables

I will do this to connect with myself in the morning:

I will do this to connect with myself in the evening:

*Now, identify one specific action you're willing to commit to this week. It might be something you are eliminating or adding to your life. It should be something specific you're committing to and willing to be held accountable for.*

One action I am choosing
to take now to honor myself
and reinvent my life is:

I acknowledge myself for:

# Self-Confidence

In order to reinvent our lives and create lasting change, we need to have self-confidence, which means we're able to trust ourselves—an essential skill we develop through the process of reinvention. But here's what's tricky—to get through life, we occupy roles, we create and maintain personas, we bend to make ourselves acceptable to others, and we get attached to the armor we develop for protection. When we live life this way, we direct our energy, attention, and efforts at trying to manage ourselves, our relationships, and the way people perceive us. We spend tremendous time and energy on constructing an identity and persona to present to the world. We diminish our self-trust in the compulsion to be something other than who we are.

Many of us do this automatically. We're conditioned to believe that we have to hide some part of ourselves in order to be loved and accepted. Maybe it's a quality or characteristic, or maybe it's something we're keeping secret, something we think would cause others to stop loving or liking us if they actually knew about it. And, at the same time, we desperately want to be loved for the truth of who we are. The disconnect here is that we can't *possibly* be loved for who we are unless we're willing to reveal who we are.

> We diminish our self-trust in the compulsion to be something other than who we are.

Remember when we were exploring self-worth, which was all about owning our wholeness, even the parts we had an aversion to? Self-confidence picks up this thread because, now that we've learned to own who we are, we can begin to embody and reveal it. Self-confidence is inherently relational. It's one thing to own our strengths and weaknesses, and it's another thing to actively, openly express them. A person who displays self-confidence is communicating, "I'm willing to be who I am and accept it without fear of judgment."

We can look at where we lack self-confidence by looking at the personas we've constructed. A persona is an identity that pushes aside parts of ourselves we don't like or that frighten us. Maybe we don't want to be needy. We don't want to be angry. We don't want to be mean. Whatever we push away, the disowned qualities we explored a couple weeks ago only become even stronger, louder, and more insistent, wreaking havoc in our lives until we choose to actually acknowledge and integrate them.

You can usually tell which qualities you are pushing away by recognizing the places in your life where you are trying to overcompensate. For example, if it's important for you to conduct yourself and be seen as someone who's fiercely independent, it's possible that you're pushing away neediness. Or, if you tend to be overly gracious and soft-spoken, it could be that you've been repressing anger. Often, we tend not to trust ourselves to express "undesirable" emotions like neediness or anger in a healthy way or in a way that will be received, which causes us to make foregone conclusions that result in limited choices about how and who we need to be.

You might take a moment now to think of a persona you've adopted. What are the roles you play in your world? These can be practical—like partner, parent, leader—or perhaps more dramatic, like rescuer, fixer, savior, superhero, breadwinner. Just keep in mind that a persona is totally value-neutral, meaning it's neither negative nor positive; it's just that you've attached special importance to it and may see it as an integral part of your identity.

Let me give you an example. I used to be obsessed with projecting an image of perfection to the world and managing the perceptions of others. I carefully gave others a very specific lens to see me through. I wanted to be seen as someone who could make anything and everything happen, without ever making mistakes. Although the toll this took was invisible to others, in retrospect, it was obvious to me. I never wanted to take risks, ask for help, try new things, or even be wrong. As such, all of my actions were premeditated and orchestrated. It was very difficult for me to be in the moment and act spontaneously, as I didn't want to leave anything up to chance. I spent an inordinate amount of time concocting my responses to the world. For example, if I was in a room full of people and we were taking turns going around the circle to share, I would completely miss out on everything people were saying—because I was so concerned about how I would respond and come across to others. It was exhausting! Not to mention, it was difficult to connect with other people because I was overly concerned with how they would perceive me.

> **We can't possibly be loved for who we are, unless we're willing to reveal who we are.**

This pattern of rejecting ourselves is actually an old, old habit from childhood. Remember, we were raised to package ourselves to be digestible to others. We were trained and conditioned as children in our families and in our schools. When we were young, before our logical thinking minds were developed enough to process the experiences around us, we received messages from our families and our teachers about what was okay—and more importantly, not okay—to be.

Maybe your teacher called you bossy. Maybe your mother told you how lazy your neighbor was. Maybe your dad complained that you were just too much. Wherever it came from, all of us received similar messages, and we obeyed. We decided that certain aspects of ourselves were unacceptable—to be avoided, disowned, and dismissed. And we pushed them away. We whittled away at the wholeness that is our birthright. The wholeness that is essential to our sense of self-worth, as we discussed a couple weeks ago.

Many of us still spend a lot of energy pushing away the things we don't want to be, pushing away whatever we think is negative; we fail to realize that every characteristic or trait exists inside of us for a reason and that every single part of us comes bearing gifts. When we push away a quality we don't want to be, it will refuse to be denied. We create chaos to avoid telling ourselves, and others, the truth. And of course, when we do that, the truth comes out sideways. One of my mentors, Debbie Ford, often described this phenomenon as similar to holding a blown-up beach ball underwater; at some point, it pops up with full force and hits you in the face. The built-up pressure that comes from denying your truth will often do the same thing. At some point, something's gotta give.

I experienced this as well when I was unhappy in an abusive marriage but didn't want anyone to know the truth. Of course, because I was addicted to perfectionism, I hid behind the facade of a perfect marriage that I projected outward, manipulating what people perceived. I had an affair because I couldn't bear to tell the truth, even to myself. I betrayed myself and my marriage. When my now ex-husband read my journals, the truth came out sideways—and it was painfully messy.

So, what compels us to stay inside our inauthentic shell knowing that it takes such a toll? Because we get something from it. We see some benefit, some payoff. And we're afraid of what will happen if we let go of these payoffs and benefits. Such payoffs and benefits include:

- Not having to take a risk (and possibly fail!)
- Never having to feel rejected
- Remaining in a cocoon of comfort (even if it means playing it safe and staying small)

It's important to know that it will feel easier to stay small and imprisoned rather than face the uncertainty of becoming who you are meant to be. It's time to challenge that impulse—because in order to keep yourself in the container of the persona you've constructed, you will have to slip into denial, numb out, and stuff down your real feelings and your true self. The only way out of that is *self-forgiveness*.

## The Power of Self-Forgiveness

One of the things you should know about the process of reinvention is that nothing we've done in the past to hide parts of ourselves is "wrong." If we experience difficulty revealing the full scope of who we are, of the infinitely rich world that lives within us, it's because we haven't learned to accept our true selves.

**Self-acceptance comes from self-forgiveness.**

Self-acceptance comes from self-forgiveness, which can feel strange to those of us who are used to judging ourselves. Self-forgiveness is about forgiving ourselves not just for our perceived mistakes, but also for the qualities within us that we feel ashamed of.

When we withhold self-forgiveness, we withhold self-love and self-acceptance. Self-forgiveness practice is an essential element of reinvention and often requires more attention than forgiving others, since most of us are much harder on ourselves than anyone else.

It won't help us progress to expend energy on regret, to beat ourselves up for something that happened in the past, or to constantly

> **When we withhold self-forgiveness, we withhold self-love and self-acceptance. Self-forgiveness practice is an essential element of reinvention and often requires more attention than forgiving others, since most of us are much harder on ourselves than anyone else.**

bludgeon our so-called imperfections. Instead, we can be compassionate to ourselves and recognize that all these painful feelings are what lead us to build personas—and, as a result, to feel shut off from the wild, messy, infinitely interesting world around us . . . which is full of lots and lots of people who are probably doing exactly the same thing!

When we recognize that our armor and personas are just part of our ingenious self-preservation, we can gently set them down once and for all. We can finally forgive ourselves.

Often, we operate under the mistaken assumption that self-forgiveness isn't possible—that *someone else* needs to give us the stamp of approval before we can be assured that we're actually okay as we are. But this is placing the responsibility on someone else to validate us rather than sourcing our own power from within.

Other times, we externalize our forgiveness, believing that if we forgive someone else—a neglectful partner, a critical parent, or an unsympathetic boss—we'll experience the sense of relief and release we've been waiting for all our lives. Truly, the only person we really need to forgive is our own self! In fact, it's futile to even contemplate forgiving someone else unless we've wholeheartedly forgiven ourselves.

One thing that's helped me practice self-forgiveness is the recognition that our whole lives are made up of a vast array of experiences. When we label one as "good" and another as "bad," we forget how they're all so intricately connected. On the one hand, I could look at my affair as something I regret, something I have to forgive myself for—on the other, I can honestly see it as the greatest gift of my life, because it inadvertently led me down a path that took me to the career I have now, which I wouldn't have even considered otherwise!

Self-forgiveness expands our own story about our lives, which includes our sense of purpose and what we truly love. When I openly reveal the story of my affair, I no longer need to cling to the story that I'm a bad person for having cheated on my ex-husband. I can see past the narrow prescriptions.

Of course, I'm not letting myself off the hook or giving myself a hall pass and saying what I did is great. Self-forgiveness is not the same as condoning my actions; rather, it's understanding and accepting why I did what I did. In retrospect, I can see that had I heeded my boundaries and listened to the voice that told me not to get married, I wouldn't have put myself in a position to then betray myself, first and foremost, and my marriage. Today, through the lens of compassionate self-forgiveness, I am aware that the circumstances for which we most need to forgive ourselves directly result from crossing our own boundaries. With

> **Self-forgiveness is not the same as condoning my actions; rather, it's understanding and accepting why I did what I did.**

this awareness, it's unlikely that I will ever engage in the same behavior again.

Often, we beat ourselves up over something that happened in our past or present, and we fear that forgiving ourselves will just keep us stuck in that same behavioral loop. In truth, self-forgiveness is the antidote to the experience. It frees us from shame and hiding. It allows us to bask in our wholeness and the learning that emerges from our so-called mistakes. It gives us the conviction to move forward in the world and reclaim our voice and power. It gives us the kind of wisdom and perspective that help us to live in the world exactly as it is, and as we are. In short, it gives us self-confidence—not the kind that has us living up to the expectations of the world around us, but the kind that comes from authentically owning who we are and finding comfort and joy in our own skin. This is the kind of self-confidence that makes certain people so enjoyable to be around—because they clearly have love for themselves, they exude a nonjudgmental warmth that others can feel.

Until we release ourselves from the constraints of roles, personas, and self-judgments, on some deep level inside, we will know that we cannot be trusted, by ourselves or anyone else. When we think we have to hide behind false fronts and be someone other than who we are, we rob ourselves of our self-confidence. But when we do free ourselves from our personas, we can cultivate the innate seeds of self-forgiveness, self-trust, and self-confidence that reinvention requires.

There's a poem by Anaïs Nin called "Risk" that beautifully illuminates this: "And then day came, when the risk to remain tight in a bud was more painful than the risk it took to blossom."

Taking the risk to blossom reaps enormous rewards. When you tap into your own self-trust and self-confidence, it amplifies into trust and confidence in other people, the conditions and circumstances of your life, and the universe itself.

# day 1

The roles I play or personas I portray in my world are (list as many as you can think of that feel relevant to the person you are today):

_____

_____

_____

_____

_____

_____

_____

_____

_____

_____

_____

_____

_____

_____

_____

_____

_____

# day 2

The ways I package myself to be digestible to others are:

_____

_____

_____

_____

_____

_____

_____

_____

_____

_____

_____

_____

## The strategies I use to feel in control of situations or relationships are:

_____

_____

_____

_____

_____

_____

_____

_____

_____

# day 3

The adjectives that my acquaintances, coworkers, and colleagues would use to describe me are:

1. _____
2. _____
3. _____

The adjectives that I would use to describe myself are:

1. _____
2. _____
3. _____

The adjectives that my immediate family, close friends, and loved ones would use to describe me are:

1. _____
2. _____
3. _____

My response to these three lists is:

_____
_____
_____
_____
_____
_____
_____
_____

# day 4

The restrictions I feel
as a result of the identity
I put out into the world are:

_____

_____

_____

_____

_____

_____

_____

The true parts of me that are
longing to be expressed are:

The cost of crafting and
maintaining these roles and personas is:

_____

_____

_____

_____

_____

_____

_____

# day 5

What I most need to forgive myself for and release is:

_____
_____
_____
_____
_____
_____
_____
_____
_____

**The gift, lesson, or life wisdom that this experience I need to forgive myself for was meant to deliver to me is:**

_____
_____
_____
_____
_____
_____
_____
_____

# day 6

What's possible and available for me in my life when I forgive myself and stand in the truth of my wholeness with confidence and courage is:

_____

_____

_____

_____

_____

_____

_____

_____

The action I will take this week to integrate, embrace, and cultivate the self-forgiveness, self-acceptance, and self-confidence that is mine for the taking is:

_____

_____

_____

_____

_____

_____

_____

# day 7: end-of-week reflections

## My Experience of Self-Confidence

**This is what I experienced when exploring self-confidence over the last week:**

_____
_____
_____
_____
_____
_____
_____
_____
_____

I was surprised by:

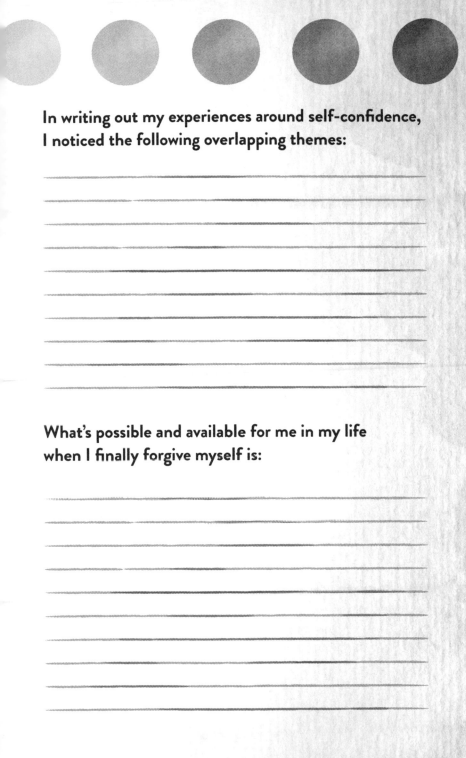

In writing out my experiences around self-confidence, I noticed the following overlapping themes:

_____

_____

_____

_____

_____

_____

_____

_____

_____

What's possible and available for me in my life when I finally forgive myself is:

_____

_____

_____

_____

_____

_____

_____

_____

_____

# self-honoring & non-negotiables

I will do this to connect with
myself in the morning:

I will do this to connect with
myself in the evening:

*Now, identify one specific action you're willing to commit to this week. It might be something you are eliminating or adding to your life. It should be something specific you're committing to and willing to be held accountable for.*

**One action I am choosing
to take now to honor myself
and reinvent my life is:**

**I acknowledge myself for:**

# Visibility

Before we dive in, let's celebrate the culmination of everything you've explored up until this point! You unearthed your vision in Week 1; calibrated by acknowledging your incompletions in Week 2; identified limiting beliefs (and replaced them with empowering ones) in Week 3; reclaimed your wholeness and self-worth in Week 4; considered what you were saying "yes" and "no" to, as well as how you might be trespassing your own boundaries, in Week 5; got a handle on your deeper unconscious commitments, as well as the power of conscious choice, in Week 6; and learned how self-forgiveness can be a potent gateway into self-confidence in Week 7. And now, the cherry on top of this entire reinvention process is the opportunity to flourish in visibility, which is our anchor for our final week!

So, what exactly is visibility? It's the permission we give ourselves to be seen for the truth of who we are, without tamping ourselves down or packaging ourselves to be digestible to anyone else; without hiding behind our beliefs, roles, personas, and any remaining stories that hold us back. It allows us to come full circle back to the original vision we identified in Week 1, and to recognize that we have the power to embody that vision through our words, our deeds, our actions, and our very *being*.

Embracing visibility is about owning your glow and focusing the spotlight on your truth. We often hear catchphrases like "step into your light" and "own your power," but visibility is so much more than a bumper-sticker mantra. First off, I want to make the fine distinction between visibility and allowing yourself to be seen. Visibility is the way we consciously shine our own light upon ourselves. It's not just that we're letting ourselves be seen by others; it's that *we're actually making ourselves visible*. We're making ourselves glow and stand out. We're doing the thing that so many of us feel is forbidden: we're drawing attention to ourselves.

I invite you to breathe into your heart, into your presence, here and now. Take a moment to pause and simply give yourself permission to invite the power of visibility in; allow it to radiate its light within you.

To allow yourself to be visible is to be an agent of your own freedom rather than standing passively by and waiting for someone else to include you in the beam of their approval. Visibility is not about permitting someone to see you; it is, however, about rightfully taking up space and letting yourself shine from the inside out, whether someone else is taking notice or not. But believe me—this kind of courageous reclamation of your light is very likely to garner results in the world around you!

The more you allow yourself to be truly visible, the richer, more genuine, and more intimate your connections and overall life will be. If any of what I've written here is filling your stomach with butterflies—some of excitement, and perhaps some of anxiety—you're not alone. The truth is, many of us were conditioned as children to dim our light. We were taught that it's not okay to

**Embracing visibility is about owning your glow and focusing the spotlight on your truth.**

> **To allow yourself to be visible is to be an agent of your own freedom rather than standing passively by and waiting for someone else to include you in the beam of their approval.**

claim the aspects of ourselves that are unique, beautiful, and worthy of applause and attention. In many ways, we were trained to disown not just the qualities we view as negative, but the very ones that define our essential goodness.

We've already explored the qualities and aspects of ourselves that we've rejected and denied because we've labeled them bad, wrong, or negative. So, this week, we're looking for the qualities we've pushed away that we'd label good, right, or positive.

In the same way we push away qualities like *lazy* or *needy*, we also push away qualities like *courageous* or *creative*. We do this because we may have received feedback that we were *too much*, instead of *not enough*. We have received messages like: "Don't be too loud." "Don't show off." "It's not ladylike to brag." "Be seen and not heard." "Don't get too big for your britches."

Maybe we lost friends when we did well in school, or we thought we couldn't be happier than a depressed parent. Whatever happened, we made unconscious decisions to reject entire parts of ourselves and contain the sparkly, vibrant stuff of our authentic self. We made a decision to hide because we were convinced it wasn't safe to shine so bright . . . to be so loud and expressive . . . to draw so much attention . . . to take center stage in our own lives and do so with exuberance and gusto.

Sometimes, without consciously realizing it, we continue to make ourselves small, invisible, and silent. Even if we long to break free and come into the light (perhaps even curating our social-media feeds to reveal our vulnerability), we secretly believe there are other parts that would cause the world to recoil from us, perhaps in envy or disgust. So, instead of savoring the compelling range of our unbridled self, we shut down. Unconsciously, we shift who we intrinsically are in a recurring reaction to whatever is happening outside of us. We bob and weave around our most amazing qualities just so we can stay safe, loved, and accepted—even if the face we are revealing to the world is mostly a hollow representation of our untamed spirit . . . meaning nobody ever gets the pleasure of knowing the true us.

So, how do you know if you're dimming your light? Below are some of the most common ways I've seen it happen:

- Not voicing your opinion if you think it's going to be unpopular or invite conflict

- Instead of accepting a compliment, deflecting or brushing it off

- Making yourself invisible or dismissing attention when it's rightfully placed on you

- Downplaying a promotion, accomplishment, or financial gain

- Feeling fearful of intimidating someone else (especially if you're in a position of authority and feel guilty about it)

- Hiding beneath excess weight or clothing, or other methods of concealing your brilliance and beauty

Something might already be bubbling up for you around the ways you personally dim your light . . . the ways that you have made the decision—consciously or unconsciously—to not be *too much* of something. Take a moment to pause here and consider one way you've taken attention off of or diminished yourself. Trust me, we keep doing it all the way through childhood into adulthood. You might not realize it, but you're probably doing it right now.

There are many insidious reasons we choose not to be visible. In fact, some of us might even see this as a virtue. We might tell ourselves, *It's time for someone else to shine*, or *I don't have anything meaningful to share, so I may as well stay on the sidelines for now.* We might admire another person or place them on a pedestal as we choose to hunker down in the audience and watch from a safe distance. We might even view our hesitation as humility, or our transference as generosity. But often, our choice to stay invisible comes from the need to hide because we believe it'll keep us safe.

However, visibility is not a zero-sum game. We don't need to remain in the shadows just so someone else can have their moment in the sun. In order for others to shine their light, we need not dim our own. In fact, our willingness to be visible can help us demonstrate to others that there's plenty of room on this particular stage.

## Taking Back Our Projections and Our Power

One of the most common methods of seeking the safety of invisibility is deflecting our light and positive qualities, and projecting them onto others. We do this because being with our own greatness often goes against our conditioning or feels overwhelming

Here's how it works: When you see someone you admire, or want to emulate, or feel inspired by (or even feel envious or jealous of—so be sure to pay attention to those pricklier feelings!), that person is likely embodying a certain quality you've rejected in yourself and pushed away. It's good to pay attention to such moments, because they are conveying vital information—information meant to remind you that everything you see in someone else is available to you.

The truth of the matter is, that quality is yours. It's in you. Remember, one of the core tenets of the reinvention process is that each of us possesses every quality and trait that exists in the universe. Yes, that includes all the bright, shiny qualities! All the things you want to be, but don't think you are—those qualities are yours too. There is nothing you can see in someone else that you are not. So, whatever lights you up in someone else is yours to take back—especially if it's a trait that might be lying dormant within you. That other person doesn't need you to be casting that which is yours upon them. You might have closed it off inside yourself at a very young age because the messaging was being imprinted upon you that it wasn't good, safe, or nice.

We internalize a lot of the judgments that come at us, beginning in our early childhood and going all the way into adulthood. We continue to seek validation externally and to mirror back the expectations other people have of us. We continue to look outside of ourselves for a source of energy or power. But of course, everything we need is inside us already! We simply need to give ourselves full permission to access it.

Think back to the moon analogy we explored during the week on Self-Worth. Although the different phases of the moon might fool us into believing that the parts we see are all there is, we know that the entire moon is *always* there, whether we can see it in its entirety or not. This goes not just for the parts of ourselves we'd rather shut down and off—it also goes for the parts of ourselves that are bright and beautiful but that we've chosen to see as belonging to others instead of to us. Our wholeness encompasses the power we might be refusing to own in ourselves, and it's up to us to reclaim it.

So, now it's time to start accessing the parts of yourself where you hold the most power. I like to define our superpowers not necessarily as those characteristics that mark us as somehow special or extraordinary, but as the qualities we've projected onto others that we haven't acknowledged we already have! It is our job to activate those dormant or underappreciated qualities within ourselves, as this is what gives us power.

Ultimately, power is energy. We usually whittle away what power we have on trying not to be something (whether that something is "too much," "not enough," "too bossy," "too needy," fill in the blank with your own version!), instead of resourcing that precious energy and acknowledging our truth from the get-go!

> **We don't need to remain in the shadows just so someone else can have their moment in the sun.**

What I found most shocking when I was at the height of crafting my "perfect" persona was that once I was able to drop the armor, I had so much more energy. When we are simply living in what's true, it doesn't take a whole lot of effort. Sure, we often think it will—but as it turns out, the greatest energy zap of all is hiding. It takes a lot of energy to hold up the weight of the armor and to remain in the belief system that we are inadequate as we are, so we have to be something we're not.

When we are no longer willing to stay in that limited belief system (which takes so much unnecessary work), we become free. And truly standing in our own power is the greatest freedom of all!

In the past couple years, I have noticed a lot of well-meaning people suggesting that I go out on dates to meet someone new. But I'm not particularly interested in the narrative that I'm inadequate because I'm not in a relationship. In fact, I rather prefer my life this way! There is great freedom in being able to let people perceive me however they want to, without attaching any credence to their ideas or allowing them to shape what I believe about myself. But getting here required being in a place where I could finally trust my own adequacy, once and for all. I had to get to a place where I was simultaneously able to deflect the negative projections people had placed on me, and to take back the positive projections I'd placed on others.

Owning your power is all about maintaining a strong vessel, such that you are no longer expending unnecessary energy or letting it leak away in sneaky, unnoticed ways. This literally frees you up to use your energy as you wish. It enables you to see that you are your own power source—so you can be free from fearing judgment . . . from feeling you need to be what someone else wants you to be . . . from molding your truth into something it isn't.

**Truly standing in our own power is the greatest freedom of all!**

I invite you to take a moment here to feel what it's like to stand in your power. Pause to celebrate the changes you've already made. Really feel how the dimensions of reinvention have supported you so far. Acknowledge yourself for what you're already creating. Embrace the changes you've made, even as you are still becoming.

Now, imagine out in front of you the being you love most in the world. This can be a person who is alive or someone who has passed. It can be an animal. Imagine that your heart is opening up and you are sending love from your heart to theirs. Feel that love in a way that is visible. Let yourself see it. Maybe it's heart-shaped confetti, or a rainbow. Maybe it's clouds, streamers, a beam of light; whatever it is, see the love you have for the being you love most in the world pouring out from your heart and going directly into theirs so they can feel and receive it.

Now, just imagine that person stepping aside, and that same stream of love you're sending out is now ricocheting and boomeranging in space back into you. You already sent love out to the person you love most—and now, the same love with the same potency and power and energy and capacity is coming back into you! Just let it permeate your entire body, so you can take your own love in, allowing it to fill every cell of your being. Breathe into the buoyancy inside of you, as you are now filled with this much love.

Take a moment here to anchor in the feeling: what it's like to allow yourself to receive your own love—and this much of it!

146

I want you to know this is available to you at all times. Anchoring in your self-love is a powerful way to take back your own energy and use it to build your power and freedom. When you allow yourself to bask in its glow, without holding back, you allow yourself to be truly visible. And there is nothing more breathtaking than that!

# day 1

What I desire in my life but am still putting off because it requires me to be more visible is:

_____

_____

_____

_____

_____

_____

_____

_____

_____

_____

_____

_____

_____

_____

_____

_____

_____

_____

_____

_____

# day 2

The superpower—or positive quality I most need to embrace—that already lives within me and that I know I need to embrace in order to step into my visibility is:

_____

_____

_____

_____

_____

_____

_____

_____

What's possible for me if I really own my superpower is:

_____

_____

_____

_____

_____

_____

_____

_____

# day 3

What I need to release in order to fully embrace
my superpower is:

# day 4

I'd like freedom from:

_____
_____
_____
_____
_____
_____
_____
_____
_____

I'd like freedom to be, do, or have:

_____
_____
_____
_____
_____
_____
_____
_____
_____

# day 5

This is what not being free costs me:

_____

_____

_____

_____

_____

_____

_____

_____

_____

**What being free, and taking back my projections and power, makes available to me is:**

_____

_____

_____

_____

_____

_____

_____

_____

_____

_____

_____

# day 6

What's possible and available for me in my life when
I finally give myself permission to be visible is:

_____

_____

_____

_____

_____

_____

_____

_____

The action I can take to step into visibility is:

_____

_____

_____

_____

_____

_____

_____

_____

# day 7: *end-of-week reflections*

## My Experience of Visibility

**This is what I experienced when exploring visibility over the last week:**

_____

_____

_____

_____

_____

_____

_____

_____

_____

I was surprised by:

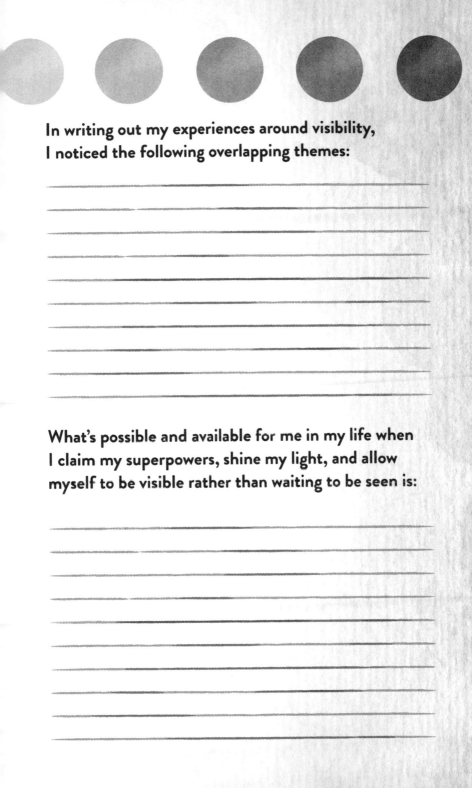

In writing out my experiences around visibility,
I noticed the following overlapping themes:

_____

_____

_____

_____

_____

_____

_____

_____

_____

What's possible and available for me in my life when
I claim my superpowers, shine my light, and allow
myself to be visible rather than waiting to be seen is:

_____

_____

_____

_____

_____

_____

_____

_____

_____

# self-honoring & non-negotiables

I will do this to connect with myself in the morning:

I will do this to connect with myself in the evening:

*Now, identify one specific action you're willing to commit to this week. It might be something you are eliminating or adding to your life. It should be something specific you're committing to and willing to be held accountable for.*

**One action I am choosing
to take now to honor myself
and reinvent my life is:**

**I acknowledge myself for:**

# Send-Off

Congratulations, you've officially made it to the end of this journal! Except . . . I hope you know this isn't really the end. In fact, it's just the beginning! You can move (or dance, or saunter, or ecstatically leap) through the eight dimensions of reinvention many times over. You might even want to pick up additional copies of this journal for yourself—and your loved ones. I guarantee you'll discover something different every single time.

The art of change is an ongoing, ever-evolving process that allows us to refine and rearticulate our vision to ourselves—and to step even more boldly into our wholeness. So consider this a bright red door that has just been flung open into the rest of your life!

My hope is that you will continue to revisit the process of working with the eight dimensions of reinvention—perhaps exploring different aspects of your vision or expanding your understanding of how your beliefs impede or support you. Whatever the case, you will certainly find that your experience and responses to the journaling prompts deepen over time, offering you greater clarity about who you are and what you're capable of. You'll also discover that each of the eight dimensions becomes more seamlessly integrated into the very fabric of your life. (And let's face it, we all need reminders!) The way you move through your world, interact with the people around you, and set goals will be affected in minor and major ways.

In general, if it isn't already obvious, I'm not a huge fan of the word *closure*. Certainly, I think it's wise to bring a cycle to completion, which is why I decided to create an eight-week journal that offers a solid container for you to recognize and celebrate the changes you've made in that period of time. However, I think it's helpful to draw an analogy from the world of mountain climbing here. In mountain climbing, there's something known as a pitch, which is a section of rock that can be covered with a rope of average length meant to protect and support the climber. In order to summit a mountain, a climber typically goes through several pitches. You can apply that analogy to our process here. You have officially completed the first pitch. (Yay!) That doesn't mean you've reached the ultimate summit, or that you have discovered everything there is to know about the art of change. Healing and growth don't occur in one straight, linear shot, but through a process that's more like a spiral. Sometimes we're *ascending* and sometimes we're *descending* on that spiral.

I want to define these two ideas for you. In a process of *ascending*, we're rising out of our own self-consciousness, self-obsession, or preoccupation with the past and our individual experience of it. In an ascending process, we are able to rise up and feel free and unburdened, untethered by the things that have historically held us down. An ascending process can be extremely exciting, as it offers more obvious experiences of transformation and pattern-dissolving for many people.

On the other hand, a process of *descending* requires digging deep and excavating different aspects of your past and long-standing patterns in your life. This process can often feel more internal and quieter. However, it's not as if ascending is better than descending, or vice versa. Both are integral (and you might find that you're doing both simultaneously, depending on where you are on your healing journey). However, many people will discover that the heights to which they rise are determined by the depths to which they are willing to dig in order to understand and honor themselves.

So, on top of the fact that each successive return to this journal might surface a new issue you would love to give laser focus to, you'll likely also discover that you are in a fresh cycle; perhaps while you were previously in a descending cycle, of digging deep into the origins of your beliefs about your self-worth, this time around will find you in an ascension process that encourages you to boldly embrace a life unencumbered by the past. You will most likely alternate between elevating and excavating!

It's so empowering to know that every single experience of moving through the art of change will be unique. And over time, as you keep coming back to it, you'll have the opportunity to chart your own progress and journey—and recognize exactly what you're growing out of and who you're growing into. It's a beautiful way to keep a living record of the person you are becoming. Remember, we are always whole in and of ourselves—but the journey of stepping into that wholeness is an adventure of a lifetime that never really ends.

I'm so proud of you and grateful for the time you've spent moving through *The Art of Change*! May you continue to shine your light brightly, today and always.

# About the Author

Nancy Levin is a master life coach, podcast host, and best-selling author of five books including her latest, *Setting Boundaries Will Set You Free: The Ultimate Guide to Telling the Truth, Creating Connection and Finding Freedom*. She is the founder of Levin Life Coach Academy, offering in-depth coaching, training, and certification programs, and has coached thousands of people to live life on their own terms by making themselves a priority and setting boundaries that stick. Nancy was the Event Director at Hay House for over a decade and received her MFA in Creative Writing and Poetics from Naropa University in Boulder, Colorado. She continues to live in the Rocky Mountains.

Website: www.nancylevin.com.

# Hay House Titles of Related Interest

*YOU CAN HEAL YOUR LIFE*, the movie,
starring Louise Hay & Friends
(available as an online streaming video)
www.hayhouse.com/louise-movie

*THE SHIFT*, the movie,
starring Dr. Wayne W. Dyer
(available as an online streaming video)
www.hayhouse.com/the-shift-movie

•••

*THE GIFT OF GRATITUDE:*
*A Guided Journal for Counting Your Blessings,*
by Louise Hay

*LIVING YOUR PURPOSE JOURNAL:*
*A Guided Path to Finding Success and Inner Peace,*
by Dr. Wayne W. Dyer

*THE COSMIC JOURNAL,*
by Yanik Silver

*THE HIGH 5 DAILY JOURNAL,*
by Mel Robbins

All of the above are available at your local bookstore,
or may be ordered by contacting Hay House (see next page).

•••